Diamonds Lost in the Sand

DIAMONDS LOST IN THE SAND
Gems of Wisdom for Educating Our Children

David Freeman

DIAMONDS LOST IN THE SAND

© Copyright 2015 — David Freeman

All rights reserved. This book is protected under the copyright laws of the United States of America. No part of this publication may be reproduced, stored in a retrieval system or transmitted in any form or by any means, including electronic, mechanical, photocopying, recording or otherwise, without the prior written permission of the copyright owner, except by a reviewer, who may quote brief passages in a review.

This book may not be copied or reprinted for commercial gain or profit. The use of short quotations is permitted and encouraged.

Design by LifeVoiceQuest.com

ISBN : 978-1-9998755-1-0

For worldwide distribution. Printed in the United Kingdom

Contents

Endorsements
Preface
Introduction

Chapter 1 — Vision 13

Chapter 2 — Diamonds Buried in the Sands of Time 21

Chapter 3 — Which Inheritance Contains the Real Diamonds? 35

Chapter 4 — Wisdom ... the Lost Diamond 45

Chapter 5 — Daniel and the Diamond 59

Chapter 6 — The Multifaceted Diamond 71

Chapter 7 — The Kingdom of Love in the Classroom 79

Chapter 8 — Every One a Gem 89

Chapter 9 — The Diamond Creator 99

Chapter 10 — Mining for Diamonds 109

Chapter 11 — Wisdom in Discipline. 119

Chapter 12 — The Diamonds in Their Setting 135

Chapter 13 — Life in the River 147

Chapter 14 — Fruit 153

Appendix 1 — Wisdom Quiz. 159
Appendix 2 — Values. 165
Appendix 3 — Keys for Wisdom in Curriculum 167
Appendix 4 — Outline Truths for Use in Lessons. 183
Appendix 5 — Unconditional Acceptance. .199
Appendix 6 — Keys for Wisdom in Character 205

About the Author

Endorsements

Do we need another book about education? A fair question but having read David Freeman's 'Diamonds Lost in the Sand' I would have to say that we need this one. This is not simply another trendy take on the educational process that leaves us crying out, 'The Emperor's got no clothes on'. No, what distinguishes the contents of this book from many others is that David has taken a view of life shaped by his Christian faith and asked the question, how does this inform my practice as an educator? If that were all that he had done it would be interesting enough but David's experiences over many years as a teacher, Headteacher and trainer of teachers across four continents give practical rigour to the conclusions that he has drawn.

In this book there is a lot packed into a small space. Not so tightly packed as to be indecipherable, but undoubtedly thought-provoking. Principles are expounded and examples offered where those principles have been successfully applied. I have known David for many years, I have watched him live out these lessons in his work and along with many others I have been a beneficiary of his wisdom. My suggestion is this; enjoy this book as you would a good meal. Savour the contents, consider the flavour, chew it thoroughly and digest it slowly. When that is done, the goodness contained within it will begin to be evident in your own life and work, then both you and your pupils will reap the benefits.

> *Graham Coyle, National Leader (England) of Christian Schools' Trust*

David— "a man after God's own heart". That's how the Bible describes the shepherd boy who became a great king.

Over the many years I have been privileged to know, observe and learn from David Freeman, this is what I have seen. He is a man who has captured and sought out the heart of God, especially in regard to education. But more than that he has sought after the wisdom of God. This book brings together a sparkling array of diamonds. These diamonds have been sought out. The whole of his life thus far has been used faithfully, sacrificially and in a great labour of love to find these diamonds of unimaginable worth and show them forth, so that you and I can be deeply enriched and enhanced and walk with greater understanding and insight, learning the lessons of wisdom within the pages of this tremendous book.

David is a man of great wisdom, knowledge and insight who carries an amazing ability to father, disciple and teach those who would desire to walk in Kingdom truth. He is used greatly both in this nation and in other nations, and he has a wealth of experience, as a teacher, a principal, a father, a minister and a teacher of teachers.

I recommend not only the book, but the man who is behind its pages, and thank him and his dear wife Rosie for the years of investment they have laid down into the lives of many, including my own family and I. Thank you.

Paul Hubbard, oversees Bradford Life Church in England and serves churches in Italy, Nepal and USA

David Freeman, who was a pioneering headmaster in a Christian school in Oxfordshire for many years, recounts how we dig for wisdom amidst the confusing array of perspectives on offer in today's world. Importantly, his educational views are not fancy theory, but well proved in the practice of teaching. He understands God's world, God's word, and how we communicate these things to children in the classroom. He has seen many lives transformed by the power of love and the communication of the whole of life in the context of God's creative activity. His insights are tried and tested. Doors are opening to him to share them in many educational contexts, where people are hungry for answers to the questions life poses.

Steve Thomas, Senior Pastor of Salt and Light International Ministries

Preface

Real Diamonds in Real Sand!

In September 1973 my wife Rosie and I were invited by friends for a caravan weekend by the beach at a place called Brean Sands. All went well until we played a game of ball on the sand dunes. Suddenly, my wife gave a cry. Both her wedding and engagement ring had come off and were lost somewhere in the sands.

In shock, we immediately hunted the area, but to no avail. Naturally, my wife was deeply saddened by the loss of her gold wedding ring and her engagement ring which was a cluster of diamonds. We returned home with heavy hearts.

At this time, neither of us had made a commitment to faith in Jesus but we had started attending a church. A plan began to form. Due to our work commitments it would be four weeks before we could return but we both felt willing to go back and search. It seemed crazy but we felt it was worth a try.

Over the next few days, unknown to each of us at the time, we both began to pray: 'God, could you help us find the rings—or at least one?'

Armed with sieves, buckets and spades we drove the couple of hours back to Brean Sands leaving our toddler with Rosie's parents who thought our plan was an impossible task. We found the sand dunes we had played upon. Fortunately, the tide never came this high so we felt there was hope. We marked out a couple of squares on the sand where we thought the rings might have fallen and divided them into vertical lines. We decided that we would only search the first few centimetres of depth. On our knees we began a laborious search up and down, sifting the sand through our plastic sieves. Some students passed by and asked if we had lost something. We told them it was a month ago. They clearly thought we were crazy! Well, perhaps we were. After an hour and a half I was on the last vertical strip of the second square. Suddenly, there in the plastic sieve was sitting

Rosie's wedding ring shining up at me!! I yelled; we jumped and laughed and hugged. "Let's keep searching", I said. "Perhaps the engagement ring is nearby." Within five minutes there was the engagement ring, sparkling in the sun! We laughed aloud. At just that moment the students returned from their swim and were amazed at our brilliant news.

Afterwards, I confessed to Rosie that I had prayed my first real asking prayer to God. "So did I!" said Rosie. We looked at each other and were filled up with gratitude. It was a miracle and God had answered our prayers! Rosie had her engagement ring made a little tighter and is still wearing both rings more than 40 years later!

Introduction

How did you feel when you finished school? Were you relieved that exams were over? I know this was my own experience. For years afterwards, I had a recurring nightmare that I had forgotten to prepare for a major exam and in my dream I was feverishly attempting the impossible task of ploughing through weighty text books because the exam was the next morning!

Sadly, I suspect like many others, I was only too pleased to walk away from the school educational process. I was full of fragmented portions of knowledge—some History; some Maths; some Science experiments; some English, etc. But I had no sense of how it all fitted together; no overall cohesive picture. I call this educational approach the 'blunderbuss approach', after the name of an old fashioned gun which had a wide-funnelled barrel and discharged a scatter of pellets to pepper the target. Many of us were showered with a wide array of disjointed facts and experiences but lacked an overall understanding of how it fitted together. I believe we have been cheated of the educational inheritance of knowledge and truth that God wants for us.

Have you only ever seen education in secular terms?

Have you been working in the dark without the overall plan or vision to help you?

Do you feel confused by conflicting pressures and demands made of you as a teacher?

God's call to us is a call back to wisdom and to a personal relationship with him for both students and teachers in the education process. It is a call back to his original plan. God's desire is expressed in Isaiah 54: "all your children shall be taught by the Lord, and great will be your children's peace."

This book is an attempt to focus on the 'diamonds' that can easily get lost in the sands of daily life. These gems are biblical truths and principles which will help us as teachers of God's children to train them for relationship and function in God's kingdom. Like hidden gems they need to be searched out. "It is the glory of God to conceal a matter and the glory of Kings to search it out." (Proverbs 25:2)

Most of the principles in this book were searched for and worked out by my team and me in a Christian school. Of course, we were only re-discovering truths that educators of the past had already revealed but they had become covered by the sands of time. Some principles, we did not discover till later e.g. the deeper and greater understanding of grace in discipline. Some of the principles I have discovered and developed through dialogue with my dear mentor Dr. Dow Robinson (who has now gone to share in the joy of the Lord who he served with such devotion). I thank God for him, and for my pastor Steve Thomas, who promoted this vision with such faith. Many thanks to the area leaders of Oxfordshire Community Churches who had faith, stood with us, prayed and worked with us—often physically! I also thank God for my colleagues of the pioneering first years at The King's School in Witney, Oxfordshire. Without you the school could not have been successful. Thank you, Julia Morgan, Vera Rodgers, Keith Elmitt, John Ellwood, Leila England, Wendy Rapson, Mary Dunlop, Cathie Jones, Debbie Newman, Hazel Carter, Joan Ford, Colin and Sheila Green, Julie Purnell, Anthea Dillon, Linnie Campbell, Mary Pim and Libby Dobson. You all walked with me in those early years of the school, worked with great commitment and shared the journey of revelation, which has been the inspiration for this book.

David Freeman July, 2015

Chapter One

Vision

Can the God who made the snail have also made the leopard? Can the one who created the vast, starry galaxies have also created the ant? God's creation is full of astounding contrasts and so are his plans—they are staggeringly cosmic and yet intricately individual. God delights to work from the small to the larger and he is never in a hurry!

The Diamond in the Context of God's Greater Plan

The Kingdom of God began to become physical reality on earth when just one tiny baby was born into an apparently unimportant family in an insignificant town called Bethlehem. Outwardly Jesus' birth didn't appear to signify anything at all of cosmic relevance. But, for those who were searching, the truth was revealed: the baby was God's son! God frequently seems to disguise what he is doing, even making it unattractive at times, so that only those with the right inward attitudes and motives discover it.

In order for us to be effective co-labourers with God, we must be searching for the right thing with the right heart attitude, otherwise we shall miss God's purposes for his children in education. Jesus' command to us is: "Seek FIRST the kingdom of God and his righteousness" (*my emphasis*). What is the kingdom of God? How do we seek it? The word 'kingdom' (in Greek: *basileia'*) is an unusual word because it is a verb–noun! It is a noun that is active! It is not a physical territory but the active rule of the king through our hearts and lives. Theologian George Ladd explains that 'the meaning of *basileia* cannot be reduced to a single concept but is a complex concept with several facets. Its root meaning is the reign or rule of God.... The most distinctive fact in Jesus' proclamation of the Kingdom was its present inbreaking in history in his own person and mission.'[1] Bible teacher Mike Beaumont concurs, expressing it in simpler terms: 'We need to translate it as 'rule', 'sovereignty', or 'dominion'. It is not so much the place ruled as the act of ruling. The kingdom is, then, a rule before a realm. One day it will be a realm—a definable 'place'; but not yet!'[2]

I recently heard a preacher define the gospel of the kingdom in very simple terms. He said that it is all about a father and his son and their family business. Throughout the Bible, beginning in Genesis, we see God's desire as a king and a creator to have a kingdom family who would fill the earth and reflect his glorious image.

God addresses Adam and Eve:

"God blessed them and said to them, 'Be fruitful and increase in number; fill the earth and subdue it. Rule over the fish of the sea and the birds of the air and every living creature that moves on the ground.'"[3]

The Meaning of the Word 'Education'

What has all this to do with the process of education? Everything! We are mistaken if we perceive education as a separate entity in itself rather than a process which is part of the larger context of God's Kingdom. The word 'educate' comes from the classical Latin root *educo*: to educate, put in, lead or draw out.[4] There are two verbs with similar meanings. The most common verb used is *educere* (a 3rd conjugation) which means to draw out, lead out; also to rear, bring up with reference to bodily support particularly. The other verb used is *educo-are* (a 1st conjugation) which means to bring up, rear, educate (usually refers to the mind)

---

1 G.E. Ladd: A Theology of the New Testament, p.68
2 M. Beaumont: The Future Starts Now! p.11 (Roots and Shoots Series)
3 Genesis 1:28
4 A Latin Dictionary Lewis and Short OUP 1969 impression (First edition 1879), p.627

nourish, support, produce, train. It is obvious that neither Latin verb specify *where* the pupil is to be led or the goal of the training. The goal is up to the educator. By contrast, God the Father has very specific goals for his children, yet those goals are part of a greater cosmic plan. Perhaps the metaphor Jesus used of himself as a shepherd King who leads his flock to fresh pastures[5] is applicable here in a Christian view of education. The Christian teacher is working with parents to lead pupils to explore the wonder and wisdom of God and his creation and their role in it.

Throughout the Old Testament there is a continual emphasis from God regarding the importance of teaching our children the truth about God's revelation of himself and his wise instructions for life.

Abraham

Abraham is chosen by God circa 1900 BC to begin a whole new nation which was to demonstrate faith in God. It is interesting to note that Moses' account in Genesis informs us that God valued Abraham and chose him because he would teach his children faithfully:

"For I have chosen him, so that he will direct his children and his household after him to keep the way of the Lord by doing what is right and just, so that the Lord will bring about for Abraham what he has promised."[6]

We are also told that Abraham had 318 trained men who had been born in his household.[7] Clearly, Abraham was into education of some sort!

Joseph's Royal Egyptian School

After the challenging years of rejection, slavery and imprisonment under false charges, Joseph is raised, through his ability to explain Pharaoh's dream, to become his prime minister in charge of the whole nation. In this role, Joseph was

---

5 John's Gospel Chapter 10
6 Genesis 18:19
7 Genesis 14:14

entrusted with the education of Pharaoh's young princes and also of Pharaoh's elders.

'He made him master of his household, ruler over all he possessed, to instruct his princes as he pleased and teach his elders wisdom.'[8] Like every ruler, Pharaoh valued the education of the next generation to perpetuate his dynasty through superior wisdom.

The Plan Progresses

Throughout all of these developments, God's greater plan is progressing. The Kingdom of God, although freshly inaugurated by Jesus, is evident in the Old Testament (although somewhat hidden). In Judaism, there is a regular theme of God's kingship: he is King of Israel but also King of the all the earth.[9] The Psalmist proclaimed God's sovereign kingship: 'The Lord reigns, he is robed in majesty … Your throne was established long ago. You are from all eternity.'[10]

Once delivered from their subsequent slavery in Egypt, Israel was called to be a special kingdom of God's people. God says: "Although the whole earth is mine, you will be for me a kingdom of priests and a holy nation."[11]

Much later in Israel's history, during their exile in Babylon, the interpretation of King Nebuchadnezzar's dream is given to Daniel. It is the revelation foretelling the Kingdom of God which would overcome and outlast all other earthly kingdoms and would fill the entire earth. 'In the time of those kings, the God of heaven will set up a kingdom that will never be destroyed, nor will it be left to another people. It will crush all those kingdoms and bring them to an end, but it will itself endure forever.'[12] N. T. Wright explains in his insightful book about the kingship of God: 'The Jews assumed, on the basis of their strong creational theology, that the creator had made the world in such a way as to be properly ordered and run by human beings. The Jewish vision of theocracy, of God being

---

8 Psalm 105:21-22
9 G. E. Ladd: A Theology of the New Testament, p.58
10 Psalm 93:1-2
11 Exodus 19:5-6
12 Daniel 2:44

in charge, was always one of a rule mediated through his image-bearers, that is, through human beings.'[13]

The World's Largest Desert School

In this section we will return to look more closely at the Israelites after their deliverance from Pharaoh. Moses surely has the most challenging role of all in leading a newly formed nation and educating their children. At the final census, the total number of the men of Israel is recorded as 601,730.[14] We can only imagine how many thousands of children are represented amongst this number, all of whom needed education to learn and live out God's laws—and in military training too.

Repeatedly, throughout Deuteronomy, Moses reaffirms God's emphasis of the vital importance that Israel should teach the next generations. "See I have taught you decrees and laws as the Lord my God has commanded me, so that you may follow them in the land you are entering to take possession of it. Observe them carefully for this will show your wisdom and understanding to the nations … Only be careful, and watch yourselves closely so that you do not forget the things your eyes have seen or let them slip from your heart as long as you live. Teach them to your children and to their children after them."[15] This emphasis is repeated again and again in subsequent chapters.[16]

Sadly, Israel was going to frequently fail in their calling to be God's special kingdom people. Perhaps one of the saddest portions of the Bible is found in the book of Judges Chapter 2. Here we are told that, after the death of Joshua (the faithful leader of the people of Israel after Moses): 'another generation grew up, who knew neither the Lord nor what he had done for Israel. Then the Israelites did evil in the eyes of the Lord and served the Baals. They forsook the Lord, the God of their fathers, who had brought them out of Egypt.'[17]

Was it, perhaps, because the Israelites were so busy taking the land that they

---

13 N. T. Wright: How God became King, p.169
14 Numbers 26:51
15 Deuteronomy 4:5-9
16 See Deuteronomy 6:4-7; 11:1-21
17 Judges 2:10-12

neglected to educate their children in the knowledge of God, his word and his ways? That unfortunate generation grew up in ignorance and subsequently degenerated into idol worship and civil war. Here is a sober warning, if only it would be heeded, for our present day. It is a great injustice that children in many schools are being denied knowledge of the word of God as a manual for life. They are also denied the knowledge of God as a loving Father and Saviour. It is an injustice because they are not being given the opportunity to make their own choice out of knowledge.

In Deuteronomy we also find the famous traditional monotheistic prayer which starts: "Hear O Israel: The LORD our God, the LORD is one."[18] N. T. Wright explains that: "when rabbis prayed that prayer they spoke of it as 'taking upon themselves the yoke of the kingdom'."[19] They were claiming God as king and his sovereignty over the whole earth.

Jewish Education

'The primary purpose of education in Bible times was to train the whole person for lifelong obedient service in the knowledge of God…The aim of learning was holiness in living…the fundamental goal of Jewish parental instruction was to transmit an historical and ethical heritage.'[20] Jewish education in later centuries centred, as always, around the family. Both parents were the first educators. Early years' education centred around the mother who provided moral education: "Listen, my son, to your father's instruction and do not forsake your mother's teaching."[21] As boys grew to manhood they were entrusted to the father's training. Roland de Vaux explains that 'One of his most sacred duties was to teach his son the truths of religion…and to give him a general education…'[22] The father's education was also to pass on his trade or crafts. The child would also learn at the sanctuaries (as Samuel did) or the temple at Jerusalem, as Jesus did when a boy. Whilst prophets and teachers of the Law gathered pupils there seems

---

18 Deuteronomy 6:4
19 N. T. Wright: How God became King, p.266
20 M. R. Wilson: Our Father Abraham, p.279-280
21 Proverbs 1:8
22 R. de Vaux: Ancient Israel: its life and institutions, p.49

to have been no organised structure of schools until the New Testament period. 'The word 'school' (*bêth–midrash*) occurs for the first time in the Hebrew text of Sirach: 51:23. According to Jewish tradition, it was only in A.D. 63 that the high priest Joshua ben Gimla decreed that every town and village should have a school which all children would have to attend from the age of six or seven.'[23] This latter ruling applied only to boys. Education was firmly the parent's responsibility.[24] The teacher is a representative of the father, according to Jewish tradition. To this day, orthodox Jews have maintained the teaching of their scriptures and their worldview to their children in the family setting, especially around the Sabbath meal. There is no doubt that a family unit can still be the most effective teaching environment where teaching can be conveyed within a relationship of unconditional love.

The importance of teaching children God's truth is emphasised in 96 AD when St. Clement of Rome first used the term 'Christian education'. The chief concern of such early Christian leaders was that the truths of the faith were to be passed on for the purpose of individual salvation and that the moral laws of Christ's teaching be imbibed to produce a properly Christian society. It was intended that parents and the church would share the task. As the church developed, teachers were employed to teach the religious instruction.

Over centuries, the diamonds of Christian education as part of the Kingdom of God would frequently be buried in 'the sands' of different cultures. In the next chapter we will explore how two main opposing philosophies emerge and conflict: each intending to represent truth.

---

23 R. de Vaux: Ancient Israel: its life and institutions, p.50
24 A.J. Heschel: The Insecurity of Freedom, p.54-55; quoted in Wilson: Our Father Abraham, p.279

Chapter Two
Diamonds Buried in the Sands of Time

In early cultures which had no experience of the true God, ordinary man was viewed as the slave of the ruling classes. If education was provided it was to serve the economic interests and success of the king or ruler who, in turn, made offerings to his gods to importune their favour. Evidence of one of the earliest known civilisations was discovered in Mesopotamia. 'Mesopotamian culture portrays human beings as almost incidental to creation, inferior beings made to serve at the whims of the gods to satisfy their personal needs. Genesis, in contrast, puts man and woman at the peak of creation and involves them in the freedom and power to determine—and spoil—all the rest.'[1]

Two Family Lines

The effect of the fall of Adam and Eve (which we will examine more thoroughly in subsequent chapters) resulted in two lines of descendants: a godly line represented by Abel and an ungodly line represented by Cain, the first murderer. Genesis tells us that Cain's descendant Lamech, a revengeful murderer, became the first bigamist and polygamist.[2] Cain's line became humanists who were determined to live by their own rule and who built the tower of Babel as a monument to themselves. They illustrate self-determinism and the progress of man in his

---

1 P. Yancey: The Bible Jesus Read p.36
2 Genesis 5:28

own pride and strength. They said, "Come, let us build ourselves a city with a tower that reaches to the heavens, so that we may make a name for ourselves and not be scattered over the face of the earth."[3] This was in direct opposition to the purpose of God which was for men and women to spread over the earth as we saw in Chapter 1.[4]

By contrast, the descendants of the line of Abel, through Seth who replaced his murdered brother, included men and women who loved God, despite their fallenness, and sought to worship and obey him. Noah and his wife and family, Abraham and Sarah, Moses, David and many more are those whose stories are told throughout the Old Testament.

As we gaze down the eras of history, we see these two lines or streams conflicting with one another and enshrining opposing values and motivations. In the sphere of education there rose up witnesses for both Christian and Humanist philosophy.

---

3   Genesis 11:4
4   Genesis 1:28

Diamonds Buried in the Sands of Time

The Two Streams of History — A Brief Overview

Our Western Heritage
Two Streams

	Hebrew (Theism)			Greek (Humanism)	
BC	**Judaism**	Adam and Eve Gen 3: First Humanism		Gen 11: Humanist Movement Plato Aristotle	**Dualism Reason**
	Romans				
AD	**'Dark' Ages**	Jesus Christ			
		Pioneers	Augustine		**Grace v Nature**
1100	**Medieval Period**	Wycliffe Huss		Thomas Aquinas	**Renaissance**
1500	**Reformation**	Luther Calvin Knox Comenius		Erasmus	**(Greek and Roman Philosophy Reborn)**
	Puritanism				
1600		Milton Owen Bunyan		Descartes Voltaire Rousseau Locke	**Enlightenment (Reason Enthroned)**
	Pilgrim Fathers				
1700	**Great Awakening**	Wesley Edwards Whitfield Carey Wilberforce Shaftesbury		Kant Hegel Robespierre	**French Revolution (Idolatry of Reason)** **Secular Science (Paragon of Reason)**
	Methodism Missions Movement				
1800	**Privatised Christianity**	Spurgeon		Darwin Marx Lenin	**Communism v Materialism**
1900	**Marginalised Christianity**	CS Lewis Bonhoeffer Graham Teresa		Montessori Fromm Sartre Dewey Freud	**Technology**
	New Xian School Holy Spirit Blessing				**Postmodernism**
2000	**Extremism places faith schools under**				**Increased secularism**

In the ancient world originating from these two family lines, these two opposing philosophies, which dictate ways of thinking and knowing, grew in the western world. A Jewish perspective is expressed by David Stern. 'The philosophical underpinnings of the western world were centred on two cities—Athens and Jerusalem. The Greeks developed philosophy in a rational manner but largely at the expense of separating heart and head. Many psychological and spiritual ills stem from this separation (one can also speak of this separation as between body and soul). The Jews kept head and heart, body and soul together, and the Bible reflects this unitary view of human nature. The head has its way of knowing and the heart has its way of knowing and neither should be ignored.'[5]

The Humanist Stream

The ancient Greek philosophers like Socrates, Plato and Aristotle pursued knowledge searching for the ultimate reality. They were searchers for truth but without God. Homer is regarded as the educator of Greece. He lived between the 8-9th centuries BC and promoted the education of an ideal type of man. A warrior education was aimed to produce either an efficient barbarian or a refined type of knight. This type of 'knight', who is heroic but chivalrous, is exemplified in his great poetic works: the 'Iliad' and the 'Odessey'. These are still used in independent public schools today as an example of ideal qualities. These early Greek philosophers believed this world was only a shadow of another supernatural reality. Greek idealism dominated philosophy, elevating the mind and the body. It interpreted education as largely cerebral and physical. It influenced religion in the west for over 100 years from before Christ until the Renaissance.

The Renaissance, as its name suggests, represented a re-birth of ancient Greek ideas: confidence in man, his creativity, his reasoning power and his ability to progress through his own strengths. The Renaissance in turn spawned the Enlightenment where man's pride asserted itself once again in the enthronement of reason and the dethronement of God. N. T. Wright explains it in this way: 'Once 'man had come of age' there was no room for theocracy. It was as simple as that. God was pushed upstairs, like a doddering old boss who used to run

---

5 David Stern: The Complete Jewish Bible. Introduction p.xxvi-vii

the company, but has now been superseded. He has, no doubt, a notional place of 'honour', a cosy office where he can sit and imagine he's still in charge. But nobody is fooled. The new generation is running the business now.... Thus for the European and American Enlightenment, God was superannuated to a position of totally ineffectual 'honour'.'[6]

The quest for knowledge was again based upon Greek philosophy and Greek ideas now became values. This continued to shape British education through the following centuries. It is evidenced still today in much of our public school system with its emphasis on a superior or privileged class who rely on their own strengths; physical prowess; a knightly type of honour and often nominal religion: in summary a classical education in an institution apart from family. It is not that all of these qualities are undesirable but that the code of life given by Christ is often only given lip-service and what results is largely humanistic. Stephen Vryhof [7] believes this resulted in the following educational thinking: that the school should prepare the children to serve the state; the conviction that religion is a private matter and that schooling is 'public' and blessedly value-neutral. All of this contributed to the building of a 'wall' between the church and the state and marginalised religion.

The Theistic Stream

In every age God has raised up men and women to be witnesses to his truth. The Hebrew people understood from the scriptures the importance of training the next generation in the absolute truths of God's word and the experiential history of his active involvement with their race.[8] This, of course, is in direct contrast with Greek ideas of the separation of children to be educated by the state and of the remote gods who needed to be placated in case of their anger. Marvin Wilson highlights the difference succinctly: 'The Greeks learned in order to comprehend. The Hebrews learned in order to revere.'[9] Truth for the Greeks was an idea to be cognitively explored—for the Hebrew, truth was 'an experience to be lived, a

---

6 N. T. Wright: How God became King p.33-4
7 Stephen. C. Vryhof: Between Memory and Vision: The Case for Faith –based Schooling p.45
8 Psalm 78:1-7
9 M. Wilson: Our Father Abraham p.291

deed to be done.'[10] Jewish education based solely on the Torah, was focussed on leading the learner to submit to the authority of God's word. The Jewish child was given a worldview. At 5 years of age, study of the Torah began. Little parchment rolls, made especially for use by children, contained the following portions of scripture: The Shema (Deut. 6.4-9; 11.13-21; Numbers 15. 37-41); The Hallel (Psalms 113-118); the account of the Creation, the Fall, and the genealogy from Adam to Noah (Gen.1-5) and the essence of the Levitical Law (Leviticus 1-8). Within these passages lie all the basic elements of a biblical worldview.[11] They were as follows:

- ◊ The origin of life through the intelligent act of a personal, unlimited Creator;
- ◊ The identity of man as the image-bearer of God , yet fallen through sin;
- ◊ His call to responsible stewardship over the earth;
- ◊ The supreme authority of God, and the absolute, non-negotiableness of moral law as something to recognise and accept, rather than determine for one's self.

The Pivotal Point of History

Jesus Christ entered the world and became the pivotal point of history as he revealed the very nature of God and demonstrated how life was to be lived in loving dependence and obedience to his heavenly Father. As the second, and last, Adam, Jesus had come to offer redemption and to reclaim mankind from the disastrous inheritance of Adam and Eve. He opposed all humanistic greed and selfishness and dealt the death blow to sin through his sacrifice for mankind on the cross, dying in their place for sin which was not his own. The resurrected Christ led to the New Testament church and the development of a philosophy based on the word of God.

---

10 M. Wilson: Our Father Abraham p.136
11 A. Edersheim: Sketches of Jewish Social Life p.124

Pivotal People

In subsequent centuries, men like Augustine (354-430 AD) and, later, Luther (1483-1546), reformed theological thinking. Augustine viewed education as essentially religious, preparing students to know God. He said: "Nay but let every good and true Christian understand that wherever truth may be found it belongs to its master."[12] The Protestant Reformation refused the Aristotelian view of a division between secular and sacred. Luther brought about the reformation of the church from its corrupt state and understood the importance of Christian education. He cajoled the councils of Germany to open Christian schools and said: "I am much afraid that schools will prove to be the very gates of hell unless they diligently labour in explaining the Holy Scriptures, engraving them on the hearts of youth. I advise no one to place his child where the scriptures do not reign paramount."[13] The French theologian and pastor of the Protestant Reformation, John Calvin, believed that the churches would not flourish unless they were supported with schools.

The Czechoslovakian educator Jan Comenius (1592-1670) stood against the Enlightenment heresy of his day which had given Science a wrongly exalted place, and held that Science exalted the divine majesty of God rather than threatening it. In England the Puritan movement brought about huge reforms in the late 16th century. John Milton wrote: "The end then of learning is to repair the ruins of our first parents by regaining to know God aright, and out of that knowledge to love him, to imitate him, to be like him ... I call therefore a complete and generous education that which fits a man to perform justly, skillfully and magnanimously, all the offices, both private and public, of peace and war."[14] Later, in the 18th century, John Wesley, the great preacher-evangelist and founder of Methodism, wrote in his journal on Friday 24th June 1748 that he opened a school in Kingswood, Bristol and preached there on 'Train up a child in the way he should go and when he is older he will not depart from it.'[15] It was not to prove an easy task either! Five years later in 1753 he wrote:

---

12 St. Augustine: In Christian Doctrine Book 2
13 Martin Luther: On education in History of the Reformation in the 16th Century by J. H. Merle d'Aubigné p.190
14 John Milton quoted in Recovering the Lost Tools of Learning by D. Wilson p.97
15 Proverbs 16:22

"I endeavoured once more to bring Kingswood school into order. Surely the importance of this design is apparent even from the difficulties that attend it. I have spent more money and time and care on this than almost any design I ever had; and still it exercises all the patience I have. But it is worth all the labour."[16]

The Battle Continues Today

As we have seen, there has been a battle for truth in every generation and ours is no different. We have received an ungodly inheritance from the French philosopher Rousseau who hated the church and promoted the theory of the noble savage in his influential book: 'Emile'. He promoted child-centred education. He remains a source of inspiration in teacher-training courses today despite the fact the he lived a debauched life and forced his mistress to give away all of the five children she bore him.[17] One asks what right he has to teach us about education!

In more recent years the American philosopher John Dewey (1859-1952), who was sometimes called 'The Father of Progressive American Education', left us another negative legacy. He promoted a humanistic and wrongly child-centred approach to education. He rejected absolute truths and promoted instrumentalism: a pragmatic approach in education. He believed that reason must be the guiding light in determining right and wrong. His book: 'Experience and Education' was a major contributory factor which encouraged the so-called 'progressive' classroom methods of the 1970s which promoted the belief and practice that the child's conduct must be governed by the child himself and that all external discipline should be reduced. Formal practices such as times tables, grammar, spelling and phonics (used in the learning of reading) were generally debunked and discarded with predictably adverse results.

Modern Wisdom?

The internet has increased our ability to gain knowledge and educate ourselves but the sources and underlying philosophy are often not discerned. Education, in every culture the world over, is seen as a passport to success and thus given prime

---

16 The Journal of John Wesley: ed. Christopher Idle p.127
17 Paul Johnson: Intellectuals p.21

importance in preparing the future generation for life. Yet in its 'wisdom', worldly authorities in their educational planning continue to ignore the very One who is the author and creator of life. It is a fact that, in many schools, it is not permissible to teach the Bible as ultimate truth or Jesus as the true Saviour/rescuer of the world. Our post-modern society has thrown out all absolute values as restrictive and detrimental to health and freedom. More than this, in recent years there has grown an intolerant hatred by many of anyone claiming to promote Jesus Christ's words: that he is the only way to know the true Father God. Secular society demands the promotion of the glory of man as his own answer to life and allegiance to the theory of evolution. Multi-cultural society demands a multi-cultural 'mish-mash', a 'pot-pourri' of faiths and non-faith, leaving children mis-led, bewildered and confused. Jesus is reduced to one of many gods or another 'good 'man; or he is ignored altogether. In addition, gender has now become the issue of debate. For a gradually increasing number, one's biological birth-state no longer determines sexuality. In our society we now have an 'i-world' where self reigns supreme.

How did this come about? Can anything be done to rectify this? Does God have a plan for education?

God's Plan Is the Answer to Modern Culture

God is a long-term planner. In these days, God is calling us back to his great educational plan. In his plan everything hinges on Jesus Christ for 'in him all things hold together.'[18] As we throw away the king-pin of creation, it is small wonder that, in the post-modern society, we have evidence of things falling apart. Leonard Cohen expresses it in a prophetic song called 'The Future'.

> *"I've seen the future, brothers:*
> *It is murder.*
> *Things are going to slide in all directions.*
> *Won't be nothing,*
> *Nothing you can measure anymore.*

---

18 Colossians 1:17

*The blizzard of the world
Has crossed the threshold
And it has overturned
The order of the soul."*[19]

What a picture of the post-modern society without the grace of God! This graphic song tells us that order in the world is lost; there is no fixed point of reference nor is there any absolute security. Things are going to slide in all directions because 'the order of the soul' has been overturned; resulting in chaos. Only in Jesus do all things hold together.[20]

A Cosmic Context

Father God's desire was the creation of family through Adam and Eve as governors of his planet earth. After their fall he sent his one and only Son to rescue and restore us to our true identity. 'For those God foreknew he also predestined to be conformed to the likeness of his Son, that he might be the firstborn among many brothers.'[21] Unless we see education within this cosmic context, we shall be teachers with limited vision and miss the treasure of the Kingdom of God which is hidden in this field. Jesus is 'the firstborn among many'—in other words he is the fore-runner, the pioneer of both our salvation and our lifestyle. We, who believe, along with the children we teach, are called to follow his example in knowing the Father and living for him.

The next verse in that chapter of Romans goes on to explain that we have a 'calling', that is, a destiny planned for us by Father. 'And those he predestined, he also called; those he called, he also justified; those he justified, he also glorified.'[22] What a wonderful future awaits each of us! God has called us individually to be justified through Jesus' sacrifice on the cross. Through his forgiveness we can be released from the sin factor (both our genetically inherited sin and our own wilful sin choices) in order that we may be 'true children' of a loving Father God.

---

19 Leonard Cohen: The Future
20 Colossians 1:17
21 Romans 8:29
22 Romans 8:30

What a tremendous experiential truth for children to make their own! What hope this gives to them and to us their teachers: that it is possible to change from the habits and patterns that bind us through the genetic inheritance received through the fall of mankind from the destiny God intended!

There Is Hope!

I remember a teacher gloomily lamenting the waywardness of a pupil and saying: "He'll never be any different; after all, it is impossible for a leopard to change his spots." What a thrill it is to be able to joyfully contradict that gloomy prognosis with the truth that through Christ all things are possible, for when we put our faith in him the old has gone and a new creation has come.[23] I have seen so many wonderful changes take place in pupils who have put their trust in Jesus and asked him to be the guiding Lord of their life. The sinful genetic code is interrupted and broken as the Holy Spirit begins to establish new patterns of speech and behaviour in line with the genetic code of the Father and his Christ.

Dan (not his real name) came to us from a state school where the teacher had given up on him, so exasperating was he. He could not (or would not) concentrate on anything except an obsessive interest in farm machinery and was unable to make friends. He came to our independent Christian school at the age of about eight. In a vibrant Christian atmosphere Dan began to open up to God and as he did so, the rebellious nature within him changed. Through encouragement he began to overcome failure and to succeed. As he became less selfish he began to make friends. Today, Dan is a handsome, articulate young man who is standing for God with a responsible job in the media.

Not only are we released from sinful patterns of life into our true potential, but wonderful as that is, we are also to be 'glorified'. This, I believe, refers to our eternal destiny as sons of God to be heirs of the Father who will reign with him in eternity. In a promise applying to us all, the apostle Paul writes: 'Now if we are children, then we are heirs—heirs of God and co-heirs with Christ, if indeed we

---

23 2 Corinthians 5:17

share in his sufferings in order that we may also share in his glory.'[24]

Father plans to share his throne with us! This staggering concept was first revealed to the disciples at the Last Supper when Jesus began to show them some of the eternal dimensions of their destiny. "You are those who stood by me in my trials. And I confer on you a kingdom, just as my Father conferred one on me, so that you may eat and drink at my table in my kingdom and sit on thrones, judging the twelve tribes of Israel."[25] What is even more revealing is that this promise is made by Jesus in the middle of a childish dispute by the disciples over their personal ambition and rivalry. It was also made with the full prior knowledge of Jesus that, within a few short hours, his students were going to run away and fail him. Yet this account gives us hope and shows that God sees our potential and uses even our weakness and failure for his purposes. Truly the plans of the Lord are awesome.

As educators, it is all too easy for us to get bogged down in the minutia of academics and learning and forget this dimension of education as God sees it. We are preparing God's children to play their part in his great family plan—both on the earth and in eternity. Jesus outlined the mission statement for this great plan in the famous passage known as The Great Commission.[26] In fact, this is an educational plan for God's family to teach and disciple others into the truth of Jesus' identity so that the reign of his Kingdom is extended throughout the nations. This means, of course, that education should be an integral part of the church's ministry: we need to see the educational training of our children as part of the discipling process for the young of the flock. To many this is heresy. "Keep education separate from the church" they cry!

Macro or Micro?

As we explore God's big plan, Jesus, as we shall see, is given the central place. Rather than education being an end in itself, as we have said, it is meant to serve God's bigger purposes and to be the process which leads us to know the one

---

24 Romans 8:17
25 Luke 22: 29-30
26 Matthew 28:18-20

person in creation who is life. He is the one in whom our lives find their identity and purpose. The goal of education should be to gain an increasing knowledge and understanding of Jesus Christ and the world which belongs to him; not just to know about the world. Through Jesus we can then know the Father: "I am the way … no man can come to the Father except through me" Jesus said.[27] Unless we perceive education in the macro terms of relationship with a personal God and this larger context we shall fall into the secular micro thinking of the world and reduce our children's inheritance to 'a mess of pottage'.

Jesus is not only our ultimate Saviour and King; he is also our supreme example of a master teacher—a perfect role model (to be explored further in Chapter 7). Truly the plans of the Lord are much bigger and better than we expected! We have a special inheritance to claim!

---

27 John 14:6

Chapter Three
Which Inheritance Contains the Real Diamonds?

All of us appreciate the possibility of receiving an inheritance. However, there are some inheritances that bring a lot of trouble. Many of the grand houses of England built centuries ago have been bequeathed to descendants who cannot possibly afford to renovate what has become dilapidated and fallen into ruin. There is a proverb which says: "A good man leaves an inheritance for his children's children."[1] Father God had a good and wholesome inheritance for us to discover and pass on to our children, especially in the area of education. However, that inheritance became lost and a counterfeit inheritance was passed on to us. How did this happen?

In the Beginning

God is a God of wholeness who creates his plans perfectly with the end in mind from the beginning. It is staggering to read that Jesus Christ, the Lamb was 'slain before the foundation of the world.'[2] In other words, God knew before he created the world that man would sin and he had already planned to give his only Son to be the redeemer of all mankind. In Psalm 33 we read that 'the plans of the Lord

---
1 Proverbs; chapter 24:13
2 Revelation 13:8

stand firm forever; the purposes of his heart endure through all generations.'[3] God is a long-term planner. We can be sure that God has a planned inheritance for the education of his children and his people.

In the beginning of creation we read that Adam and Eve, his beloved children (the first students), were placed in a 'learning environment': the Garden of Eden. This 'classroom' was unlike any we have known! It was an outdoor classroom created with beauty and care and was to be the training ground where Adam and Eve would learn from God all about his creation. The Bible tells us Adam was to 'work'[4] (yes, work is godly!). Edward Carnell believes that Adam was the first scientist. 'When Adam was placed in the Garden of Eden, he was given something to do. He was to tend the Garden and rule over the animal kingdom. He was told, as it were, to be a good scientist: for how could he subdue nature unless he developed techniques by which nature is subdued?'[5] Adam and Eve were called to steward the garden for God. From there, I believe, God planned for them to expand their territory and gradually grow into governing the whole world through the godly children they would create.

The Bible says that God 'walked with them in the cool of the day.'[6] This could have been morning or evening or both. I believe these were times of joyful fellowship, sharing and education. Adam and Eve would share their daily experiences with their father and teacher. Daily they looked to him as their reference point. One imagines that these were occasions for many questions on the part of Adam and Eve as they imbibed the wisdom of God and gained understanding of all that he was showing them of the wonderful world he had made. They were totally dependent upon him as their source of all knowledge for he was and is the omniscient one—all-knowing and all wise. Daily they learned from God all that they needed to govern the earth and by exploring and studying all that he had created for them.

---

3 Psalm 33:8
4 Genesis 2:15
5 E. J. Carnell (1960) The Kingdom of Love and The Pride of Life p.26
6 Genesis 3:8

The Corruption of the Plan

As we have seen, throughout history there has always been an enemy who opposes God's plans. The Bible tells us in Ezekiel of the rebellion of the archangel Lucifer who was the leader of worship in heaven and who became arrogant and desired to usurp God's authority. As a result he and a third of angels who supported him were ejected from heaven. Lucifer, now named Satan (which in Hebrew means 'adversary') sought to claim the earth as his domain and from there to attack God's plan for mankind. Bill Johnson in his book 'Hosting the Presence: Unveiling God's Agenda' suggests that Satan illegally claimed dominion of the earth and that Adam and Eve were to reclaim it for God little by little, much as in the same way in which Israel under Joshua's leadership was later to reclaim the land from the Philistines.

By responding to the deliberate temptation by Satan in the guise of a serpent, Adam and Eve chose to obey the voice of deception and by doing so were disobedient to the one who made them and everything in their world. As a consequence they lost their calling to rule the earth for God and provide the godly family he so desired. Their minds became distorted by the lie they had swallowed. Believing they could somehow be gods who could rival their creator, they rejected God's call to be dependent learners and they 'fell' from the place God had given them. By obeying Satan they came under his rule—a reign of sin and death.[7] They were irrevocably stained and corrupted by sin and automatically found themselves to be enemies of God in their minds, wills and actions through this wrong allegiance.

Another devastating consequence for mankind is that through disobedience to their creator, Adam and Eve have bequeathed a genetic inheritance of a sinful nature and a fallen mind to all of us who are their descendants. Ever since the fall of mankind through Adam and Eve, Satan challenged man to be his own god. In this way mankind has been denied the truth. God's word reveals, through the person of Jesus who is truth, another greater plan for mankind's education which overcomes Satan's distortion of knowledge. This redeems the former corrupted plan. God's redemption applies not just to the mind but to the whole person and

---
7   Romans 5:12

to his destiny. Not surprisingly, God's plan has an eternal dimension. The goal of God's plan for his people is 'eternal life'. Jesus defined this very simply for us in terms of true knowledge. Eternal life, put simply, is to know God. 'Now this is eternal life that they may know you, the only true God and Jesus whom you have sent.'[8]

The unique unity which had been enjoyed by Adam and Eve with God was split asunder by their rebellious choice and a tragic division was the resulting consequence: a division between man and God and between man and man, as is made clear following Cain's murder of his brother in the subsequent chapters of Genesis. This division affected every aspect of life on earth, including the education process.

A Greek Inheritance

An echo of this division is found in the ancient Greek dualism developed by the philosophers Plato and Aristotle whereby things 'spiritual' were removed, like the gods of Mount Olympus, to a heavenly realm whilst the processes of daily life and of man were relegated to a separate 'natural' sphere. Man had no fellowship with the gods but lived in superstitious fear and placated them with offerings. This led to the division between sacred and secular as shown in the following diagram.

The gods = Sacred
Natural man = Secular

This false division still affects us today. The secular state rejects the voice of the clergy, thus marginalising the church. In education, too, the dualism persists. Education became part of the natural sphere and was therefore divorced from God and secularised which is totally contrary to God's intended purpose for it. Greek philosophy, as we saw in Chapter 2, was based upon reason and focused on the mind alone. This has become our inheritance, greatly influencing and

---

8   John 17:3

moulding our educational system, giving it the wrong bias, the wrong objectives and the wrong 'wisdom'.

A Foolish Thing Is at the Heart of Christian Education

In 1 Corinthians Chapter 1, God makes some very strong statements about the arrogance of man's educational institutions and his so-called 'wisdom' in asserting that man is the sum total of all things: "I will destroy the wisdom of the wise and the intelligence of the intelligent I will frustrate."[9] This sounds like judgement! Why is God going to do this? Because man has rejected God's gift of the perfect man, Jesus, God's son, who could have educated us into all truth. God goes on to say (with heavy irony) that since in its 'wisdom' the world chose not to know God and set his mind to oppose him, God has decided to use something that will appear foolish to the mind and to the world's eyes in order to win the world back to his original plan for it. His agent is the crucifixion of his Son which repels our educated minds and seems total foolishness: 'Where is the wise man? Where is the scholar? Where is the philosopher of this age? Has not God made foolish the wisdom of the world? ... God was pleased through the foolishness of what was preached to save those who believe.'[10] There is no doubt that for God to come in the weakness of a man's body and allow himself to be put to death by his own creation seems absurd indeed. Yet this 'foolish' thing is at the heart of Christian education and is the key to lives being restored because faith in Jesus changes the heart motivation.

As we see increasing breakdown of order in many of our inner city schools, a growing anarchy amongst many disillusioned youth, and (despite huge financial investment) limited results, could it be that God is already judging a system that pursues knowledge but rejects the one in whom 'all things hold together'?[11]

---

9   1 Corinthians 1:18
10 1 Corinthians 1:21
11 Colossians 1:17

The Last Adam

As we have seen, God's original plan from the beginning of Genesis was to populate the world with a family made in his image. In the Old Testament Adam failed the test of love and obedience to God. In the New Testament Jesus, the last Adam, tested in a desert rather than a garden, resisted the deceptive temptations of Satan and overcame his lies with truth. He demonstrated the life God intended for his creation and gathered his own class of students (most of them teenagers at the time). After three years of education through personal mentoring, Jesus re-stated his Father's original purpose. This has become known as 'The Great Commission.' In this he commanded his students: "All authority on earth and in heaven has been given to me. Therefore go and make disciples of all nations, baptising them in the name of the Father and of the Son and the Word of the Holy Spirit, and teaching them to obey everything I have commanded you."[12] This is an educational commissioning of student teachers to go and lead others out into the truth which their master teacher had first revealed to them.

The goal and purpose of the church is, therefore, to make disciples of Jesus who will reclaim the earth, stewarding it for him until he returns. This is the way in which the cosmic plan can be fulfilled. This will culminate in Jesus' return in full power and glory to the earth when 'at the name of Jesus every knee should bow, in heaven and on earth and under the earth, and every tongue acknowledge that Jesus Christ is Lord to the glory of God the Father.'[13]

The Goal of Education

The goal of education, I want to suggest, fits directly into this greater plan. The goal of education is to train children to know Jesus Christ as Lord and to know his word as truth and to be equipped that they may serve his purposes and fulfil the destiny for which he created them—as one Christian school has succinctly stated in their vision statement: 'To train children to know God and to equip them to live in the light of that knowledge.' This surely is wisdom.

---

12 Matthew 28:18-20
13 Philippians 2:10-11

I want to say very clearly that I believe the church has a responsibility to support and aid the parents in the task of educating their children—and not just on Sundays. The early church took very seriously the role of educating its children. In medieval times in our own country, monasteries were centres of learning for the nobility. Monks saw it as their God-given task to teach literacy and pass on their biblical and literary heritage to the next generation. Schools developed from abbeys and churches and were promoted by Christian reformers out of a social concern for the poor.

Our English Inheritance

In our own history the state's assumption of responsibility for education is a fairly recent development of the 19th century. Prior to this, Christian reformers had always recognised the importance of education. These men and women had opened schools for the poor (especially in areas affected by the Industrial Revolution) with the express purpose of teaching the illiterate to read so that they could know for themselves the Bible as God's word. They pioneered, labouring to promote the true wisdom of God in the light of the revelation they carried. Central to education then, was the desire for children to know God.

In 1698 the Society for Promoting Christian Knowledge (SPCK) was founded to encourage local churches to establish local Elementary schools. Christians supported these schools to aid the poor. The Bible was taught as the word of God along with related moral values.

John Wesley, like many other Christian reformers who followed him, including Robert Raikes who set up the first school in 1780 and the Quaker Joseph Lancaster, who followed him with free schools, had the revelation that education was the church's responsibility in supporting parents in the education of their children, for their children are the young of the flock. Many church leaders today fail to acknowledge such a revelation—perhaps the potential cost of providing education is a major factor which deters them.

Today it is generally accepted that education is the role of the state and to suggest otherwise is to challenge a cultural idol. However, the state's involvement with education only really began in 1870 when the state government passed Forster's Education Act. The original motivation for this was to offer financial support to the sterling efforts of Victorian Christian educators like Lord Shaftesbury. Gradually the state took over more and more control and began to dictate educational objectives, understandably making schools accountable to the government for the way the money was spent—as the saying goes: "He who pays the piper calls the tune." Within a few decades the Christian principles and purpose of these early schools became diamonds buried in the sands of godless thinking.

Religious education was originally based unequivocally on the Bible, thereby shaping moral values and conduct. The 1947 RE syllabus for Sussex is a complete syllabus for Primary and Secondary schools. It covered topics such as God the loving Father; the story of Jesus; his ministry as Lord, King, Friend, Teacher and Saviour; how to serve him; the ministry of the Holy Spirit; the story of the Bible; Israel's history and land; the Gospel, the Kingdom of God and Mission; worship and prayer, and Christian work in the modern world! What a great biblical worldview was given to those children! In the frontispiece it included the following prayer from its earlier syllabus of 1925: "Almighty God, we beseech thee to prosper the work of this school. Grant that we may learn to use all Thy gifts to the advancement of Thy glory, the good of mankind, and the salvation of our own souls: through Jesus Christ our Lord. Amen."[14] The words may be archaic but the purpose of education was clearly God-centred; note, too, how God's glory and the good of mankind have priority over us.

Within the following hundred years from these words our country changed, almost beyond recognition, to become a multicultural society and, clearly, we would want to be giving our pupils understanding of other faiths in order that social harmony and understanding may result. However, rather than maintaining a clear stance on the Christian faith, which has been the bedrock of our society for centuries and laid the foundation for a justice system that was the envy of the world, the situation has deteriorated to the stage where it is now difficult in many schools to teach the Christian faith as wholly true. Instead, the gem of truth about Jesus' uniqueness becomes buried in a quagmire of multi-faith which

---

14 Sussex RE Syllabus 1947

confuses children about the nature of truth and leads to a loss of identity, values, and morality. An oft-quoted slogan by the world is that the goal of education is to 'educate for life'. A great quality of life was the offer made by Jesus Christ: "I have come that they may have life, and have it to the full."[15] This gem has been largely buried.

Ironically, in the week I began writing this chapter, the government is calling for moral values to be re-instated! As disrespect, anarchy, violence, pornography and drugs multiply in some of our state schools and it is necessary in a few to have knife searches, the prophetic warning of Martin Luther quoted in Chapter 2, which he wrote in the 16th century, sounds dreadfully relevant. He said: "I am much afraid that schools will prove to be the very gates of Hell unless they diligently labour in the Holy Scriptures, engraving them on the hearts of youth."[16]

Generational Transfer

We cannot put all the blame on the schools or the education system, although they may have much to answer for. The government in this century increasingly emphasises the partnership role of parents. Parents, I believe, with the help of the church, have the primary biblical responsibility to train their children to know God. God is a God of generational transfer. He intends for truth about him, both through personal experience and through his word, to be passed on relationally in the context of 'family' from one generation to the next as a godly inheritance.

Christian independent schools, see their role as a partnership in faith with parents: an extension of the family in order to pass on Christian beliefs and values.[17] In recent years the Church of England schools have re-emphasised their desire for every child to know Jesus Christ. Expressing it boldly, the Report published in 2012, stated that one of their premises for all children in their schools, whether of faith or non-faith, was 'to work towards every child and young person

---

15 John 14:6
16 Martin Luther: On education in History of the Reformation in the 16th Century by J. H. Merle d'Aubigné p.190
17 See 'The Love of God in the Classroom' by Baker and Freeman. Focus Publications.

having a life-enhancing encounter with the Christian faith and the person of Jesus Christ.'[18] Sadly, in 2018, the Church of England seems to be espousing teaching from Stonewall rather than developing its own advice from a more biblical basis.[19]

Many of the present young generation are suffering an injustice through not being given the opportunity to hear in full measure about the inspiring life and wise teachings of Jesus Christ. In the majority of our state schools, they are left in ignorance of these teachings which offer a manual for life. Ideally, these need to be passed on by those who live out their faith in their own lives (as many Christian teachers of RE do in state schools). It is an inheritance that children and young people have a right to know about, whether they accept or reject it. This is not indoctrination but a child's right to know and is part of their inheritance.

Psalm 78, which records the teaching of a leader to his people, puts it like this: "I will utter hidden things, things from of old—what we have heard and known and what our fathers have told us. We will not hide them from the next generation; we will tell the next generation the praiseworthy deeds of the Lord, his power, and the wonders he has done. He decreed statutes for Jacob and commanded our forefathers to teach **their** children, so the next generation would know them, even the children yet to be born, and they in turn would tell **their** children. Then they would put **their** trust in God.[20] (Emphasis mine)

This contains some of the wisdom of God which is God's intended inheritance for us; an inheritance which contradicts and confounds the 'wisdom of the world'. In in the next chapter we will explore the nature of this wisdom and what it may mean for a God-centred curriculum.

---

18 The Church School of the Future 2012 p.9, 1.8
19 Stonewall campaigns for the equality of lesbian, gay, bisexual and trans people across Britain.
20 Psalm 78: 2-7

Chapter Four
Wisdom ... the Lost Diamond

How the gold has lost its lustre, the fine gold become dull! ...The sacred gems are scattered at the head of every street Lamentations 4:1

What you 'see' will determine what you can experience. In 'The Last Battle' by C. S. Lewis, there is a scene where the dwarves refuse to open their eyes. They believe they are imprisoned in a smelly stable. In fact, they are free and they are seated in a beautiful field on a hill but no one can convince them to open their eyes and discover their freedom. God wants to open our eyes, and to give us fresh revelation about many things that we have only understood in part or in worldly thinking. God needs to renew our minds and give us a fresh understanding of his wisdom in education. The first diamond we will seek out on the way to wisdom is the gem of knowledge. It is said that knowledge is power. What was God's intention—did he want us to have knowledge or was he withholding it from us as was suggested to Eve by Satan? Although God's adversary attempted to bury the diamonds of God's truth, they have been revealed throughout the ages to those who would seek God for true knowledge.

A Parable: The Diamond of Knowledge

A man was struggling to find direction in his life. On his wanderings he suddenly discovered a beautiful jewel lying in the dust of the street. It was a diamond, large and dazzling with many different hues. It was the jewel of knowledge. Now he had to choose what to do with it. At first he was tempted to take it for himself and place it on his own person (self-adoration). Next, he was tempted to think of all it could buy for him: he could exchange it for goods and wealth (self-improvement). As he gazed at the diamond jewel's sparkling depths of flashing colour, he was captured by it again. Like Frodo in 'The Lord of the Rings', he grappled with his emotions, which wrenched his heart at the thought of parting with such a jewel. In desperation he turned to God and was given a vision of Jesus as King. He looked to Jesus for direction and saw that the crown on Jesus' head was missing a jewel. The man suddenly understood that what was lacking was his worship of Jesus with the new revelation of the knowledge he had just gained. He could yield it to God for him to place it in Jesus' crown (worship), for there was a lack in Jesus' crown—but could he manage to do so? The struggle within him intensified. Finally, he cried out: "Help me Lord! Have your way!", and as he looked up into Jesus' face he saw that the jewel was now in Jesus' crown. Peace flooded his heart and mind. Jesus reached out to guide him on the right path which opened up before him. Now he knew the way!

What Is the Purpose of Knowledge?

1. Is it to glorify one's own ego?
2. Is it power to dominate through knowledge, outdoing others?
3. Is it power to use knowledge for evil?
4. Is it for knowledge's sake?
5. Is it to gain knowledge so that we can be like Jesus?
6. Is it so that we may 'know' God?

Knowledge belongs to God. One of his attributes is omniscience: he is all knowing. He desires to share and impart that knowledge to his people. God's purpose for knowledge was, I believe, perverted by Satan. In Chapter 3 of Genesis, we saw that Eve was beguiled by Satan, who questioned her obedience to God, and sowed doubt in her mind about God's integrity in his plans for her and Adam. As we examine this pivotal account further we can see that it focuses around the issue of knowledge.

When Eve recounts her understanding of God's command, she states, "We may eat fruit from the trees in the garden, but God did say, 'you must not eat fruit from the tree that is in the middle of the garden, and you must not touch it, or you will die.'"[1] When we examine God's actual command to Adam, it appears that Eve has added to it. The original command was, "You are free to eat from any tree in the garden but you must not eat from the tree of the knowledge of good and evil, for when you eat of it you will surely die."[2] Eve adds to the command, saying "we must not touch it". Possibly, Adam had told her not even to touch it.

Satan then deceives Eve by contradicting God, as she later acknowledges. "You will not surely die," the serpent said to the woman, "for God knows that when you eat it your eyes will be opened and you will be like God, *knowing* good and evil."[3] (my italics) By saying this, Satan perverts the true nature of God and also perverts the true nature of knowledge. He achieves this aim by firstly attacking the integrity of God, suggesting that God is withholding knowledge and experience from her because he wishes to keep things from her and prevent her development towards 'maturity'. This is an attack on the goodness of God. Secondly, this attacks the dependent, loving and learning relationship that Eve and Adam had with God. Thirdly, it is the first temptation to humanism, where man is tempted to become God. Fourthly, Satan perverts the purpose and nature of knowledge, reducing it to only knowing good and evil. God's desire is for us to gain wisdom by knowing how to relate to him.

The Purpose of the Tree of the Knowledge of Good and Evil

Why did God cause the tree of the knowledge of good and evil to be out of bounds to Adam and Eve? John Calvin, like many theologians, explains that this was a test of their love and obedience; a reminder that, although governors of the earth, they were still accountable to God and under his authority. God's desire

---

1 Genesis 3:2-3
2 Genesis 2:16-17
3 Genesis 3:4-5

was for Adam and Eve to learn out of a loving relationship with their creator, father and teacher. He wanted them to freely choose to love him by remaining obedient to his command, being willing to be dependent on him for knowledge and wisdom which they could readily access within their intimate relationship with him. This would ensure that they enjoyed life in all its fulness. He never intended knowledge to be divorced from him as a separate commodity. God himself is omniscient: all knowledge is *in* him. By disobeying God's command and partaking of the tree of knowledge, Adam and Eve now gained the awful responsibility of having to make their own decisions about what was right and wrong in any and every situation: and this without access to the wisdom available in God.

The decision to obey Satan rather than God brought them under Satan's rule and would now cause them eventually to 'die'. 'In addition, by obeying Satan, they have sinned by rejecting God's authority. God's word had promised a consequence which is a penalty: the wages of sin is death. They 'die' to their intimate relationship with God by obeying Satan and coming under his rule: 'the law of sin and death' as Paul expresses it in Romans Chapter 7.[4] They will also die physically.

When Jesus, the last Adam, came he resisted the temptation from Satan to be his own independent arbiter of knowledge and faithfully depended on God's word, quoting it without adding any of his own words or arguments. Throughout his earthly life Jesus relied on his Father for guidance, direction and knowledge. Speaking of himself as 'the Son', Jesus said: "I tell you the truth, the Son can do nothing by himself; he can only do what he sees his Father doing, because whatever the Father does the Son also does."[5]

As we saw in Chapter 3, Adam and Eve traded their rich inheritance: access to God's limitless knowledge, in exchange for Satan's deceitful promise that they can have knowledge apart from God. This is a lie, as all true knowledge is found in, and related to, God. Like the man in our parable, they were tempted to gain

---

4 Romans 7:21-24
5 John 5:19

knowledge for themselves. In our parable, which would we choose as the real purpose of gaining knowledge?

1. Is it to glorify one's own ego? Knowledge is obviously important but it can produce arrogance of character; whereas biblical knowledge should involve humility as all knowledge belongs to God.

2. Is it power to dominate through knowledge, outdoing others? Knowledge is power but this is selfishness and control.

3. Is it power to use knowledge for evil? The application of knowledge can be used for good or evil purposes, as we see in the knowledge gained by scientists in splitting the atom. However, to choose to use knowledge destructively is wickedness

4. Is it for knowledge's sake? The accruing of knowledge 'puffs up' resulting in arrogance and a spirit of superiority, the apostle Paul tells us, unless motivated by love.[6] This would be idolatry.

5. Is it to gain knowledge so that we can be like Jesus? This sounds laudable but Satan wanted to be like God too!

6. Is it so that we may 'know' God? This also sounds good but it makes knowledge utilitarian.

The parable of the jewel of knowledge shows us that knowledge belongs to God and its primary purpose is to glorify him. How can we do that? We do this by using our knowledge to worship God in all that we do. Paul, writing in his letter to the church at Ephesus, tells us that man was created for the praise of his glory. When we yield our knowledge to God by using it to serve him, we are worshipping him with our actions, and with our lives.

We may understand worship as musical adoration. The most used Hebrew word for worship *abad* (used 290 times) carries three aspects in one meaning: work, love and serve. The root of this word means to labour, to serve,

---

[6] 1 Corinthians 8:1

and this is usually translated 'the service of God'. The worship of God and the service of God are practically synonymous terms in the Old Testament. The word for worship is related to work! It does contain the idea of loving adoration of God, i.e. giving God his 'worth-ship'. However, this is a particularly English view. In the Hebrew the word worship contains three aspects of meaning: love, work and serve as seen in the following diagram.

Worship

Love

Work

Serve

Jesus summarised the greatest commandments in this way: "Love the Lord your God with all your heart and with all your soul and with all your mind. This is the first and greatest commandment. And the second is like it: 'Love your neighbour as yourself'. All the Law and the Prophets hang on these two commandments."[7]

This is worship: Loving and serving God with all your life energy; this includes your work. The word worship is first used in the story of the sacrifice of Isaac by Abraham in the book of Genesis, Chapter 22. Here it means love out of an active obedience.

In the book of Exodus where the Israelites are in slavery to an oppressive Egyptian ruler, the story is told of how God used Moses to rescue his people. Moses asked Pharaoh to let the Israelites go to worship God. Pharaoh refused. In fact, the Pharaoh requires the Israelites to worship him by labouring for him in the building of great monuments and architecture for his new city. In essence, the

---

7   Matthew 22:37-40

Pharaoh is saying "No. I want the Israelites to worship me." The issue is: who will receive the life energy of the Israelites? God desired for them to go and worship him with their energy, their lives, so that he could do them good.

So the purpose of our lives, to which true education should lead us, is to gain knowledge so that we can serve a loving God with our lives, energies and skills. This is true worship: to love serve and work for him. In this way, we will be fulfilled and the purpose of knowledge is safeguarded.

Knowledge in the World

In Genesis Satan successfully perverted this purpose of knowledge. Satan caused Eve to desire this knowledge and 'wisdom' for selfish purposes. The consequence of this sin reverberates down through the ages. Knowledge is now reduced to cerebral and cognitive knowledge by use of the mind's rational and logical processes, rather than including revelation out of a dependent relationship with God. Rational and logical processes are part of God's purpose for man's mind. However, these processes need to be submitted to the Word of God and the Spirit of God. When knowledge becomes purely cerebral, it becomes self-centred and is used by man to promote himself, and with it, gain power and control over others. Man then becomes 'always learning, but never able to come to the knowledge of the truth.'[8]

In turn, wisdom is also reduced to the application of man's intellectual knowledge and experience. Whilst this is an aspect of wisdom, the true essence of wisdom is found in living our lives in relational obedience to God and being led by the Holy Spirit, who is the spirit of wisdom. Gerhard von Rad, in his exploration of the complexity of Israel's wisdom says that for the Hebrew, '… the fear of Yahweh was the unutterable presupposition of knowledge. Inevitably, in a postmodern society that largely denies God, this has largely been lost in the learning that takes place in the world's universities today.'[9]

The Spirit of God reveals to us the truth that every part of knowledge is related to

---
8   2 Timothy 3:7
9   Gerhard Von Rad: The Wisdom of Israel p.295

God. St. Augustine famously said: "Wherever truth be found let it declare that it belongs to its master."[10] The Apostle Paul's revelation stated succinctly: 'In Him (Jesus Christ) are hidden all the treasures of wisdom and knowledge.'[11] This short sentence is a tremendous statement with huge implications for education. If ALL, not some(!), of the treasures of wisdom and knowledge are hidden in Jesus Christ, then there is no knowledge or wisdom outside of him! Let us explore how this can be revealed in curriculum and how it will lead to the wisdom God wants to impart to us and our children.

Every Subject Relates to God and His Wisdom

Every subject, I believe, represents an aspect of the knowledge of God and his world that he wants us to experience in order to lead us to greater wisdom. Every subject relates to him and is a facet of his wonderful character. Genesis Chapter 1 introduces us to all subjects of the curriculum in an embryonic way. In this account of creation there is language, mathematical order, astronomy, science, geography, history, anthropology and many more. The subjects are all integrated into the one whole creation story. In curriculum we need to remember that subjects belong to God and that they can be wonderfully integrated even while we still need to study them separately in depth. In the following brief summaries, clues of God can be seen in all the subjects.

Mathematics

Mathematics is based on the reason, order and logic with which God created his universe. In his fascinating book [12] James Nickel explores the history of mathematics and the effect of religion and philosophy upon it. He says: 'Mathematics is 1) but a tool, a servant that 2) aids man in unravelling the wisdom of God found in the harmonies and wonders of his works.'[13] Is God a mathematician? Most definitely! If he is God of creation then number was created by him and reflects his nature through its order and his eternal essence is reflected through its infinity. There is no highest number; you can always add another one! Mathematics

---

10 St Augustine: On Christian Doctrine: Book II
11 Colossians 2:3
12 J. Nickel: Mathematics: Is God Silent?
13 J. Nickel: Mathematics: Is God Silent? p.43

is challenging for the majority of children because it requires systematic logic. It also requires obedience: in order to get the answer to any problem or calculation you must follow the correct steps. How frustrated I used to become by those long multiplication or division sums where one small numerical error could make the whole answer wrong! We had no calculators when I was at school! We need patient teachers who can impart faith in the learning process!

Addition and multiplication reflect his increase; subtraction his decrease. Division represents justice and equity. Fractions represent the fact that in God's world everything, including us, is meant to be part of something larger and everything can be dissected into smaller parts. We are at once a whole person but also a fraction of a larger gathering such as our family, our class, our community or our country. 'You are all Christ's body and each one is a part of it.'[14] This scripture describes us as both a whole number and a fraction. There are many accounts of measurement and calculation in the Bible (Noah's ark, the Temple) and, of course, there is even a book dedicated to Numbers!

Science

The word Science is derived from the Latin *scientia* which simply means *knowledge*. It has come to be applied to a specific area of knowledge. God is a scientist who has created an awesome universe with amazing complexity. He is the designer of infinitesimal atoms and molecules as well as huge galaxies. Man is enabled by knowledge and wisdom provided by God to explore his miraculous creation. The great scientist, Sir Isaac Newton, famously said of the cosmos: "This most beautiful system of the sun, planets, and comets, could only proceed from the counsel and dominion of an intelligent Being. [...] This Being governs all things, not as the soul of the world, but as Lord over all; and on account of his dominion he is wont to be called "Lord God" ... [pantokratōr], or "Universal Ruler". [...] The Supreme God is a Being, eternal, infinite, [and] absolutely perfect."[15] Our science lessons should evoke the awe and wonder of God and perhaps should end in worship of such a marvellous creator.

---

14 1 Corinthians 12:27
15 Cited in Principia, Book III; Newton's Philosophy of Nature: Selections from his writings, p.42, ed. H.S. Thayer, Hafner Library of Classics, NY, 1953.

English language and foreign languages

Every language is important and reminds us of its origin at the tower of Babel in Genesis Chapter 11 when God frustrated the humanistic unity of mankind who were intent on self-aggrandisement and evil. Every language contains a structure and order in its grammar and a unique vocabulary, which, because language is spoken by the living, is always developing and changing. The learning of foreign languages is important to build relationships and cooperation. God is a communicating God who wants the gospel conveyed through language from the living to the living. How often a few words of a people's language spoken by a visitor open their hearts to that visitor and the message they carry! Learning language requires discipline and is not so attractive to a generation which has easy access through the internet in its various forms. We English joke that it is because we as a nation are so poor at learning languages that God has caused English to be the second language in so many countries all over the world!

Literature

Literature teaches us about relationships, motivations, choices and consequences. Literature is all about the power of story to engage the imagination and emotions, which Jesus used to great effect in his teaching. Literature also allows us to explore the characters of worthy heroes and the flaws of others so that we may learn vicariously about these issues and, hopefully, avoid making the same mistakes in our own lives. Literature teaches about worldview and can greatly add to our wisdom.

Art

Art is often regarded by the undiscerning as a lesser subject. In many developing countries it is almost ignored and given little or no time on the timetable. Yet art is a demonstration of the fact that we are made in God's image; as he is creative in many different ways so we can be creative. All art is primarily based on the colour and design that God used to make our world. Sunrises and sunsets, birds, butterflies, flowers, land and seascapes, mountains all demonstrate the variety of an amazingly creative God.

History

Although the glib saying: "History is His Story" may be too trite, yet it carries a truth. The Bible teaches that God *is* sovereign over the plans and affairs of mankind and the nations. As Daniel was shown in the Old Testament, God ordains seasons and the reigns of powerful cultures. Biblical history is linear not cyclical and proceeds towards the goal of the earth being 'filled with the knowledge of the glory of the Lord as the waters cover the sea'.[16] In God's plan there is a beginning and an end to history on this planet. The beginning is depicted in Genesis and the end will be when Jesus returns. History reveals the way in which man's greed causes war and confusion yet ultimately God's purposes move steadily forward. The devotional promise, 'All things work together for good to those who love God and are called according to his purpose'[17] is, in fact, an historical statement. The Bible states: 'Blessed is the nation whose God is the Lord, the people he chose for his inheritance'[18] and 'Righteousness exalts a nation.'[19] Any nation which attempts to honour God and live by his standards will be blessed.

Geography

A Christian view of Geography reveals God the creator and designer of the physical world and the provider of resources for his people who dwell in it. It involves physical and demographic geography. A key biblical passage regarding the study of Geography (and also history) is found in the book of Acts. 17: 24-27: 'The God who made the world and everything in it is the Lord of heaven and earth and does not live in temples built by human hands. And he is not served by human hands, as if he needed anything. Rather, he himself gives everyone life and breath and everything else. From one man he made all the nations, that they should inhabit the whole earth; and he marked out their appointed times in history and the boundaries of their lands. God did this so that they would seek him and perhaps reach out for him and find him, though he is not far from any one of us.'[20]

---

16 Habakkuk 2:14
17 Romans 28:18
18 Psalm 33:2
19 Proverbs 14:34
20 Acts 17:24-27

Today Geography has become a very wide-ranging subject incorporating many more concepts. The key concepts are: place, space, scale, interdependence, physical and human processes, environmental interaction and sustainable development, cultural understanding and diversity. However, modern geography now involves the study of how economies, societies and environments are interconnected. It builds on pupils' own experiences to investigate places at all scales, from the personal to the global. 'Geography inspires pupils to become global citizens by exploring their own place in the world, their values and their responsibilities to other people, to the environment and to the sustainability of the planet.'[21]

A Christian perspective explores these aspects in the light of God's creation and planning. One of the key biblical themes is stewardship of the planet God has given us; this includes how to develop the land responsibly and how to redress the negative effects of man's greed, exploitation and carelessness.

PE and sport

This aspect of curriculum is a vital area for character training as well as skills. God created our bodies to be healthy and strong. Physical exercise and pursuits are all part of stewarding our bodies and developing our strength, dexterity and skills. Athletics teaches the need for discipline in training, perseverance and pushing through physical challenges. The corporate aspect of team sports is also a key area of importance. Through these we learn how to cooperate, how to work as team, how to serve with our skill and how to aim to win but have grace when a better team excels over us!

IT, design and technology

Our society is a technological society. We need to be serving our pupils (who are often quicker than many of us!) in enhancing their skills but also in learning the right attitude to technology. In God's purposes Technology is to serve us both in accessing information and in administration, rather than ruling us. As one colleague put it: 'Go to the source of all information before going to your information source.' Design and Technology show us God the designer, the wise creator and efficient administrator; he created from nothing. He has made us in

---

[21] National Curriculum

his image and gifted some specially to design and build or create from natural resources.

RE

The study of theology, through God's word, deserves a significant place and significant time on our timetable, apart from devotional times. In RE we are educating our pupils in the uniqueness of Christianity, including ethics and morality. It is also important for them to understand alternative worldviews so that they can appreciate where others of different beliefs are coming from and relate effectively to our multicultural society. We intend to prepare our pupils to be respectful of all other faiths and non- faiths from a secure foundational base in theology. We desire for them to relate effectively and compassionately to all people. The study of other main religions is important to equip them with this understanding.

From all these curricular aspects of knowledge, we can learn principles of wisdom (see Chapter 10 for more on Christian Curriculum) and more of the fascinating nature of our God. God's aim is for us to apply our knowledge and use it to gain wisdom. In the next chapter we will explore the huge topic of wisdom further and see how this is demonstrated by Daniel in the Old Testament.

CHAPTER FIVE
Daniel and the Diamond

If any of you lacks wisdom, he should ask God. James 1:5

The more I study Daniel the more my admiration for him (and the way God used him) grows. In the story of Daniel we see the diamond of wisdom shaped and applied. Daniel was only a teenager when his world collapsed around him. King Nebuchadnezzar, whose reign lasted from 605 BC to 562 BC, had established a great empire across Mesopotamia, covering present day Iraq, Kuwait, Palestine and Syria. In 605 BC he besieged Jerusalem and deported its nobles as slaves to Babylon, his capital city; among these was Daniel. Jerusalem was subsequently to be largely destroyed by Nebuchadnezzar in 597 BC, and its walls, temple and palace were razed to the ground.

Daniel is thought to have been part of a noble, priestly family and may well have been trained towards becoming a priest. With the invasion of Nebuchadnezzar, all of these plans were destroyed and Daniel was forced to walk the thousand miles to Babylon in chains. He lost almost everything. He lost his family, his freedom, his beloved city and temple, his land and his future. In Babylon it is possible that he was castrated in order to serve as a eunuch in Nebuchadnezzar's palace. He even lost his name which meant God is my Judge, as he was re-named Belteshazzar, probably meaning in Babylonian 'Bel (i.e. Marduk) protect his life.'¹ We can only imagine the trauma Daniel experienced as a Jewish boy who had been trained to abhor idols. For the rest of his life he would have to answer to this name. He began a three year educational programme in Babylonian language, and literature—a literature full of idolatrous myths.

Although he lost so much, he never lost his faith—Daniel was well-grounded. The word of God was in his heart and he remained devoted to the true God all his life, praying three times daily facing towards his beloved Jerusalem. God also granted him his three friends, Hananiah, Mischael and Azariah. Together they would experience hair-raising exploits serving in the administration of their new king.

Nebuchadnezzar as King, although a military dictator who could be ruthless, was not necessarily always as dogmatic and bombastic as he is often portrayed. He was extremely diligent to make true and righteous judgements designed to be pleasing to Marduk, the god who he believed protected his city of Babylon. He prohibited bribery and intimidation. Few Babylonian kings attained the reputation of justice to which they aspired; Nebuchadnezzar perhaps came closer, as Neo-Babylonian texts suggest. Donald Wiseman says: "This view of him as the Babylonian king seemingly concerned with the spiritual and moral issues of life, anxious for divine guidance and working for the spiritual and material welfare of all peoples is no mere propaganda. As a contemporary record it accords with the statements in Daniel where Nebuchadnezzar is shown as willing to accept the interpretation of dreams even when these were later attributed to revelation by a god other than a recognised Babylonian deity and to whom he had attributed the title 'the most High God.'"[2]

Daniel discovered the diamond of God's wisdom amidst pain and a pagan society. His devotion to God was the catalyst as he was faced with the licentious lifestyle, food and drink apportioned to all being trained for the king's service. Meat offered to idols was prohibited to the Jewish people. Daniel courageously, yet with tact, takes a stand and wins the agreement of the chief official, Ashpenaz.

---

1 NIV Study Bible p.1279
2 D.J.Wiseman: Nebuchadnezzar and Babylon p. 101

This stand of faith against the odds is typical of Daniel; it was to be repeated many times. God's favour was clearly upon Daniel and his friends as they chose a vegetable fast. At the end of ten days they looked better nourished than the rest of the trainees and after three years they passed the end of school exams under the inspection of Nebuchadnezzar himself as state examiner with astonishing success. 'The king talked with them, and he found none equal to Daniel, Hananiah, Mischael and Azariah; so they entered the king's service. In every matter of wisdom and understanding about which the King questioned them, he found them ten times better than all the magicians and enchanters in his whole kingdom.'[3]

What was the secret of Daniel's wisdom? I would suggest there are several components. First of all, it came from being grounded in God's word and a God-centred worldview. Daniel's devotion to God is another factor, which included a reverent fear of the Lord. 'The fear of the Lord is the beginning of wisdom and knowledge of the Holy One is understanding'.[4] This enabled him to access the source of God's wisdom through the revelation and guidance of the Holy Spirit, who is called the Spirit of wisdom and truth.[5] The greatest example of wisdom through revelation came with the life-threatening order of Nebuchadnezzar when a dream from God deeply troubled him. He threatened to execute all his advisors, including Daniel, unless they could give him the interpretation of his dream. The added challenge was that they also had to discover the dream itself, because Nebuchadnezzar refused to tell them its substance! Daniel went into prayer and fasting to seek God's wisdom and God granted him the answer through revelation by the Spirit of God. This elevated him to the top administrative post for the rest of the king's reign! In this drama we see how the 'jewel of knowledge' from our parable in the previous chapter is applied through Daniel's trust and devotion to God. The knowledge form Daniel's training teaches him how to approach the king and how to articulate it with deference. The Spirit of God then gives him the appropriate response when Nebuchadnezzar bows down to worship him—an embarrassing act which Daniel would have wanted to resist but dare not in this circumstance!

---

3   Daniel 1:19-20
4   Proverbs 9:10
5   Ephesians 1:17; John 16:13

In Hebrew understanding wisdom was never viewed as merely intellectual or purely cognitive which was a Greek view of wisdom. Marvin Wilson explains that neither did wisdom have to be rational: 'He (the Hebrew) knew he did not know all the answers. He refused to over systematise or force harmonisation on the enigmas of God's truth or the puzzles of the universe … Stated succinctly, the Hebrews knew the wisdom of learning to trust in matters that they could not fully understand.'[6] Wilson goes on to explain[7] that although all wisdom came from God and began with the ability to see and evaluate all of life from God's point of view, it had practical results which came from skill in applying knowledge and understanding to a specific area—it could result in very practical action. It implied the 'know-how' or capacity to perform a particular task. It could involve leadership. In fact, one of the Hebrew words for wisdom is *shekel* which stands for wise behaviour but is also the Hebrew word for coinage! Through four successive kings' reigns Daniel stood faithful for God as the kings' advisor. His wisdom appears to be both practical in administrative government and supernatural through revelation and dreams. The latter aspect is totally unacknowledged in our education system!

How do we train our pupils in God's wisdom? Like Daniel they need to have a firm grounding in scripture (including memorisation of God's word), a biblical worldview, and a personal experience of God in worship and in daily issues; both in their personal and their school-related lives. Some of the pupils taught in our Christian school are now in their thirties but they still talk of the way God answered our corporate prayers of faith on several occasions when, as a fledgling school, we faced opposition from local government and we saw God act in our favour. Assemblies with prayer requiring God's intervention gave the lasting experience of God's answers.

Our pupils also need to understand their culture and their society. Gerard Kelly in his book 'Stretch' brilliantly explains how aspects of Daniel's experience need to be applied by us today for our pupils in a post-modern world. Just as Daniel resisted assimilation in the Babylonian world, so our pupils need to find the way

---

6 Marvin R. Wilson: Our Father Abraham p.152
7 Marvin R .Wilson: Our Father Abraham p.282-3

to release God's message and love to their generation. Kelly explores seven aspects of Daniel's faith. It was 'intrinsic' in that it was rooted in God, not externals and 'eccentric' in that it was engaged with culture but anchored beyond it in an eternal dimension. It was 'acoustic' in that Daniel teaches us to have one ear to our culture and one to God; like Daniel we need to learn the poetry, literature and music of our modern society to be able to understand its perspective so that we communicate meaningfully with it. Our pupils need an 'elastic' faith that, like Daniel's, can be stretched to endure opposition and even persecution. We need a 'kenotic' heart towards God which will pour out our lives in servanthood for him, as Jesus did. He 'made himself nothing, taking the very nature of a servant…".[8] The Greek word for Jesus' sacrifice in that verse is kenosis—which signifies an emptying out of one's self. Our faith also needs to be 'poetic', able to express itself in music and the arts to a culture that is starved of imagination and, finally, 'panoramic' in that we educate our pupils to see the big canvas of history which will give them a bigger perspective of God and his purposes.

A Lifelong Quest

Wisdom is a life-long process as we grow in our understanding of God through our walk with him. Many books have been written about it and certainly our one or two chapters can only point out some aspects of it. In his study of wisdom Dr Dow Robinson[9] explains: 'Think of wisdom as a grand and stunning house. Our 'habits' are like treasures that fill each of the many rooms within this extraordinary mansion. And each treasure-habit we deposit in a room expresses the uniqueness of God's creation in us, and the hard work we experienced to develop that habit.'[10] He continues to explore 12 facets that we can begin to acquire as habits in our experience. He takes these from Proverbs Chapter 1.[11] They include:

Admonitional instruction: the wisdom we can learn from correction which will help to mature us.

---

8   Philippians 2:7
9   Dr D. Robinson: Wisdom Quest, ACTS publications
10 *Ibid* p.5
11 Proverbs 1:2-4

Understanding: the ability to discern and distinguish, to perceive and form a judgement. The scientific method develops this, although it can only form hypotheses.

Wise behaviour: the wisdom to live our lives according to God's moral code: something the wisest King Solomon, ultimately failed to do.

Righteousness: a relational standing with God which involves integrity and godliness in the lifestyle.

Administrating justice: to bring daily affairs under the rule of what is right; to judge rightly.

Equity: impartiality, to evaluate appropriately.

Astuteness, Prudence: shrewdness (the Hebrew word used for this was 'shekel' —the same word used for money in Israel today); the ability to discern real value in a product.

Knowledge: the acquisition of facts and data rather than supposition.

Creative planning, Discretion: involving contemplation to use creative ideas to produce a new product, theory or work of art.

Persuasive Learning: to use this in sharing with others so that they embrace it.

Wise counsel: advice or guidance which steers and leads to a resolution.

Wise saying: proverb, figure or riddle; the use of metaphor and allegory or intriguing puzzle.

Daniel's life portrays many of these.

Wisdom Also Involves Consequential Thinking

Daniel, because of his understanding of the omnipotent sovereignty of his God beyond Israel, responds in a crisis with faith but also with consequential thinking. Faced with a licentious lifestyle he looks ahead and foresees the consequences. He responds out of a healthy fear of the Lord which is part of wisdom. This causes him to take his courageous stand. Acting without thinking and without consideration of the possible results of our actions can lead to folly. A colleague of mine in Africa once recounted to me that she was driving along one day on a country road when she saw a lorry coming towards her with its bonnet up! The driver was leaning out of the window to try and see the way ahead. As she drew closer, to her amazement she saw that a mechanic was under the bonnet working on the engine as the lorry drove along!

There are many stories in the Bible to illustrate the need for consequential thinking: the ability to look ahead and use some of the abilities listed above. We have the story of Jonah who should have realised the consequence of disobedience but learned the hard way! There is Naaman, whose pride almost prevented him from being healed of leprosy. It is interesting to note that twice in that story wisdom came from a humble servant. Even the godly prophet Samuel nearly missed God's choice of a new king when he was misled by the outward ruggedness and good looks of Jesse's eldest son. Fortunately, his sensitivity to the Spirit of God caused him to hear God's counsel: "Do not consider his appearance or his height, for I have rejected him. The Lord does not look at the things man looks at. Man looks at the outward appearance, but the Lord looks on the heart."[12]

Right in the beginning, when Adam and Eve are deceived into making their disastrous choice, one of the factors which beguiled Eve was Satan's appeal to her senses. He provoked her curiosity and then her senses took over. 'When the woman saw that the fruit of the tree was good for food and pleasing to the eye and also desirable for gaining wisdom, she took some and ate it.'[13]

This story illustrates a very important aspect of choosing wisely: it is not wise

---

12 1 Samuel 16:7
13 Genesis 3:6

to judge only by the outward appearance or through our senses of sight; rather, we need to ask God to guide us—to confirm or reject by the revelation of his Spirit. Abraham's nephew, Lot, made the same mistake in choosing to live in godless Sodom by the lush outward appearance of the land. Naaman was choosing wrongly because of the appearance of the river Jordan which was in flood and looked muddy. Some of the disciples judged Mary Magdalene critically because of her extravagant adoration of Jesus with costly perfume. Jesus rebuked them by saying that what she had done was totally acceptable to him and, in fact, would become famous throughout the world. How important it is to help our older pupils to beware of choosing friends or partners solely on their personal appearance. Many have rued the day they made such a choice which affected them for years to come. Wisdom is available from God if we will ask him. [14] The Holy Spirit is the agent of wisdom through Jesus Christ and can guide us with discernment. Jesus' promise was that the Holy Spirit would lead us into all truth.[15] (For a study worksheet on aspects of wisdom which can be used with older pupils see Appendix 1.)

Jesus was not deceived by outward appearances. When the crowd flattered him he was not fooled. Jesus shows us how to live in dependence on God by listening to the Holy Spirit in every situation. The Spirit of God has been given to us to 'guide us into all truth'. He is the invisible and secret agent of God's wisdom. The Spirit knows all things: 'The Spirit searches all things, even the deep things of God ... no one knows the thoughts of God except the Spirit of God. We have not received the spirit of the world but the Spirit that is from God, that we may understand what God has freely given us'.[16] What an inestimably precious gift the Holy Spirit is! We need to train our children to receive him and look for his presence and guidance in all that they do.

Children Can Learn Consequential Thinking

I believe we need to train our children from an early age to understand choice and consequence. Danny Silk in his book 'Training our Kids on Purpose', tells

---

14 James 1:3
15 John 16:3
16 1 Corinthians 2:10-12

of his experiences in applying this to his own children. He explains that we over-control our children and do not teach them to mature in the ability to make decisions. Moreover he argues that the goal of obedience is an inferior goal; rather, we need to choose to obey out of love. He promotes relationship over rule. To make the goal only obedience 'can actually be detrimental to both your children's development of personal responsibility and their perception of Father. Although obedience is an important part of our relationship with our children, it is not the most important quality ... Jesus promoted relationship above the rules. Love and relationship are the bottom line of the Kingdom, and they must be ours if we wish to establish a kingdom culture in our homes.'[17] He believes that, because we do not train our children in making choices, when the responsibility and consequences are laid on them, they then tend to react and rebel in their teens without experience of how to handle greater freedom.

One example he gives in making children face consequences illustrates the need for personal responsibility.[18] A girl disobeys her mother by smuggling her pet hamster to school in her rucksack, only to leave the rucksack behind on the school bus. When she arrives home and realises what she has done, in a panic she confesses but expects her mother to take responsibility. The mother refuses and calmly informs her daughter that she must make a choice of possible actions. The daughter is aghast as she doesn't know what to do. Having let her daughter face the consequences, the mother calmly asks if she would like her to suggest a few things. She then advises her daughter to phone the bus company, helping her find the phone number, *but not doing it for her*! I think this is an excellent approach. Only as our children are made to face the consequences of their choices *and take responsibility* will they learn to think consequentially next time. In this way parents take the role of wise advisor rather than taking over and assuming full responsibility. The hamster was retrieved safely and returned home!

The following process, 3Cs, has been developed and used as a simple way of helping our pupils make choices and decisions with some awareness of consequence. The 3Cs stand for Choice, Counsel and Consequences.

---

17 D. Silk: Loving our Kids on Purpose p.35
18 D. Silk: Loving our Kids on Purpose p.107-108

In every choice to be made we can train our children to practice like a highway code: 1st – Look up; 2nd – Look back; 3rd – Look forward.

To **look up** means to begin by asking God for his help. We then **look back** (Counsel) to gain advice from either God's Word, or mature Christians. We then need to **look forward** to Consequences, asking questions like: "Will that be pleasing to God, to my parents?" "Is this likely to lead to an activity or relationship that will not be good?" The realisation that, although we can always be forgiven by God, there are always consequences is a sobering one. Disobedience always leads to a loss of <u>something</u> whilst obedience leads to more blessing.

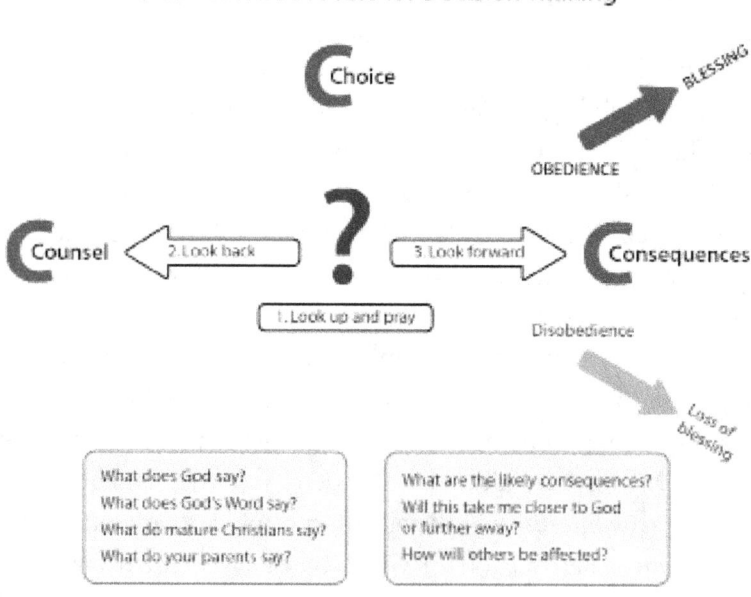

This simple approach may provide reflecting time and an opportunity for more wisdom rather than leaping thoughtlessly into action. Of course, the self-will is a strong factor which needs recognition. If our pupils can learn, even from mistakes, to yield their hearts to God, it will save them much heartache in the future. Because of his faith and because of the consequences Daniel foresaw at the beginning of his exile in Babylon, he took a stand over the rich food and the meat offered to idols; this opened the way for God to bless him with wisdom and ultimately led to the saving of many lives. This does not mean that our pupils can avoid loss and persecution. We see from the stories of Daniel in the lion's den, and his three friends who were prepared to die in the fiery furnace rather than compromise their faith, there is a cost in refusing to compromise. They were willing to lose their lives for their faith. Yet in both of those dire situations God delivers them.

Having learned from the wisdom of Daniel, in the next chapter we explore the wisdom and goodness of the God he served.

Chapter Six
The Multifaceted Diamond

When God created mankind he said, "Let us make man in our image, in our likeness ... So God created man in his own image, in the image of God he created him; male and female he created them."[1] Note that the Hebrew word for 'man' in these verses refers to both male and female. What does it mean, as parents, teachers, children, to be made in the image of God? It clearly doesn't mean that we physically replicate God's likeness but that we *reflect* and *represent* God.[2] How do we do this? The child's question (and that of many adults too!) is: What is God like? The short answer is 'He is good.' This is delightfully conveyed in the C.S. Lewis classic novels on Narnia where the four Pevensey children meet the talking beaver and are hearing about Aslan, the Lion and rightful king of Narnia who represents Jesus. They ask if he's safe: "Safe?" said Mr Beaver ... "Who said anything about safe? 'Course he isn't safe. But he's good. He's the King, I tell you."[3]

The most amazing revelation in the Old Testament of the nature of God and his goodness was given to Moses. Moses had asked to see more of God's glory and God answers by saying, "I will cause all my goodness to pass before you and I will proclaim my name, the LORD, in your presence."[4] What follows is an encounter on Mount Sinai where Moses is privileged to receive a revelation of God's

---

1 Genesis 1:26-27
2 John Calvin: Commentary on Genesis
3 C.S. Lewis: The Lion, The Witch and the Wardrobe p.75
4 Exodus 33:19

character as God proclaims it before him. It is worth quoting in full because in this short account we see the DNA of God's nature—and it is all good!

'Then the Lord came down in the cloud and stood there with him and proclaimed his name, the Lord. And he passed in front of Moses, proclaiming, "The Lord, the Lord, the compassionate and gracious God, slow to anger, abounding in love and faithfulness, maintaining love to thousands, and forgiving wickedness, rebellion and sin. Yet he does not leave the guilty unpunished; he punishes the children and their children for the sin of the parents to the third and fourth generation." Moses bowed to the ground at once and worshipped.'[5]

Let's look at each of these 8 qualities of God's character:

The LORD, the LORD—This is God's chosen name, which in Hebrew is Yahweh and is connected with the Hebrew verb *hayah*, 'to be' and means 'I Am who I AM'—the self-existent God. This is the name that had been communicated to Moses on his first encounter with God at the burning bush (in Chapter 3 of Exodus). It was an exclusive and sacred name to the Israelites who regarded it as so holy they wrote it without vowels—YHWH. It stands for his unchanging sovereign existence and authority.

Compassionate—this literally means 'God's heart is moved at the sight of suffering.' God is a kind God.

Gracious—this stands for unmerited, undeserved favour. Although we were enemies of God he still reaches out through his Son to rescue us from our rebellion.

Slow to anger—this is not just patience but forbearance: the quality of standing with the one who opposes or resists you.

Covenantal mercy—God's covenantal abounding kindness. He seeks our good, even at his own expense.

---

5   Exodus 34:5-8

Covental faithfulness—God maintains faithful love to thousands and for a thousand generations. In Hebrew the meaning is infinite.

Forgiving—literally it means 'To lift, bear our offences'. He forgives all wickedness, rebellion and sin.

Judging—God is a just judge who evaluates rightly. It is important to note that in the new covenant made through Jesus' sacrifice, we are no longer responsible for the sins of our fathers. This does not apply due to the new covenant Jesus has made, whereby we are responsible for only our own sin. In judgement God is never hasty but rather, long-suffering. In Genesis he is careful to show Abraham that he will not bring judgement on Sodom and Gomorrah without due care.[6] All God's judgments are just and right because he alone sees and knows the hearts and deeds of all mankind. He waited until the right time in history to send his Son, who would face God's righteous judgement which had been stored up over centuries because of man's sin. At the end of time Jesus will be the judge of the whole earth.[7]

Jesus Was the Exact Representation of God's Goodness

Jesus, when he became a man, was made in God's image. 'The Son is the radiance of God's glory, the exact representation of his being'.[8] Jesus shows us what Father God is like—he both represents him and reflects his character. The apostle Paul wrote to the Colossian church that Jesus is the image of the invisible God.[9] Jesus himself said to Philip and the other disciples, "Anyone who has seen me has seen the Father".[10]

As a son is like his father, so Jesus carries the same DNA as his Father God. Therefore, all the qualities revealed to Moses should be seen in Jesus.

---

6   Genesis 18:20
7   Revelation 20:11-15
8   Hebrews 1:3
9   Colossians 1:15
10 John 14:9

Authority
Does Jesus have authority? Indisputably! We see his authority in his teaching; over storms; demons, sickness and ultimately death. His authority amazed the people who heard him.

Compassion
Jesus showed compassion on many occasions: to the crowds when they had nothing to eat; to the widow whose son had died; and to the lepers.

Graciousness
'Jesus was full of grace and truth'.[11] In spite of his own holiness, Jesus had grace for the needy and the sinful, the prostitutes and the cheating tax-collectors. He spent time with them and ate with them. His ultimate grace for all mankind was shown on the cross.

Slow to anger
Jesus rarely became angry. When he did it was unlike our anger in that it was not uncontrolled and was not on his own account but on account of his Father. He became angry when he saw the pollution of his Father's 'house' (the temple) and, in a considered act, he drove out the swindlers cheating the poor through extortion. Mark (who wrote his Gospel in conjunction with Peter: an eye-witness of these events)[12] tells us that he visited the Temple on one day to ascertain what was happening. He returned after prayer the next day to restore it so that it would be aligned with his Father's intention for it to be a place of prayer rather than a market for dishonest business. The anger of Jesus showed self-control on another occasion. He challenged the hard-hearted legalism of the Pharisees who opposed him for healing the man with the withered arm on a Sabbath in the synagogue. He doesn't shout, or lose his temper but challenges them with a question.[13]

Covenantal mercy
Jesus shows God's mercy to many: the leper, the poor but especially the woman

---

11 John 1:14
12 Mark 11:11-19
13 Mark 3:1-6

caught in the act of adultery[14] who should have been stoned by Jewish law. Mercy trumps judgement, reflecting his Father's mercy. Jesus saves her and tells her to go and sin no more.

Covenantal faithfulness

Jesus was a faithful elder son to his family over many years until he was thirty. He provided for his family after his father Joseph died. He was faithful and committed to his disciples to the end; and after his resurrection. He never gave up on Peter, although he had denied and disowned Jesus emphatically three times. It was the same for all his disciples who remained after Judas had committed suicide following his betrayal of Jesus.

Forgiveness

There is hardly any need to record that Jesus demonstrated to the very fullest measure the forgiving nature of his Father; most fully when the nails were being driven into him on the cross. He prayed "Father forgive them, for they know not what they do."[15]

Judgement

Jesus says that the Father has entrusted all judgement to him as the Son.[16] While on earth Jesus showed compassion and mercy to many, including the woman caught in adultery, but judged the teachers of the law and the Pharisees, for their hypocrisy,[17] for they were leaders oppressing God's people.

If we have been born again into God's family and received Jesus Christ then we are his children. The Holy Spirit will be forming in us these same qualities. We have the potential to reflect and represent the nature of Father God in our lives, the God in whose image we are made. These characteristics are to be our inheritance. How do they translate into the educational scene for those of us who are teaching or heading up schools?

---

14 John 8:3-11
15 Luke 23:34
16 John 5: 22
17 Matt.23:13-15

Godly DNA in a School Setting

In a school setting we are called to model Christ as much as he enables us to do so. We are to reflect and represent him as those made in his image. What might this look like?

Authority

We have authority but how are we demonstrating it? We need to know that if we have followed a call from God into teaching, we have his authority to fulfil the task. 'The one who calls you is faithful'.[18] In a school, as a teacher, we are under the authority of the headteacher. As headteacher we are under the authority of the school governors or school board. Note that the authority of God is followed by the next quality of 'compassionate'. Is our authority harsh or is it kind and considerate (whilst still being firm)?

Compassionate

Do we have compassion and kindness for all, especially the deprived or inadequate pupil or those with special needs? This is the heart of God. It is important to realise that many pupils with learning difficulties work harder than some of the more gifted children and need our kindness and reward.

Graciousness

Are we full of grace to those who don't deserve it? Of course, it is important that there is justice and fairness in our dealing with all pupils. However, are we allowing the Holy Spirit to direct us with grace on the occasions that he chooses (which we might not be quick to recognise!)? We need to stay prayerful in the midst of the many different challenges that meet us every day and listen to his prompting, especially in matters of discipline (see Chapter 11).

Slow to anger

How short or long is your temper fuse? We are all different but God wants to create in us the self-control produced as a fruit of the Holy Spirit. To be sure, our anger will not achieve anything apart from making us more exhausted and damaging relationships. I remember sadly a number of occasions when I blew

---

18 1 Thessalonians 5:24

it with pupils—it never worked for good. Much more effective was a measured and calm response with time given, where possible, to reflect before acting.

Covenant mercy
Mercy is the quality to be shown in issues of justice. More will be said about this in Chapter 11. We need a consistent, committed loving kindness in order to build positive relationships with our pupils—this will enhance their learning. It is not an easy task to give loving kindness to all pupils! This is where we call on God to give us his one-way love for the sometimes unlovely!

Covenantal faithfulness
Perseverance is the word that comes to mind here. Our commitment to our children should be expressed with faithful perseverance. Faithfulness is required in planning lessons, in trying to ensure individual needs are regularly met wherever possible. Faithfulness in marking, day in and day out, is equally important. Marking carefully and thoroughly, giving constructive feedback is time-consuming, but so important. To have their work unmarked and unnoticed is de-motivating for pupils; whilst, by contrast, our marking either honours and recognises the effort they have put in, or calls them up to face their lack!

Forgiveness
Peter asked Jesus how many times was he to forgive those who wronged him. He thought seven times was a generous amount.[19] Jesus probably blew his mind by answering 77 times! It is possible to translate this as seventy times seven![20] In other words, endlessly! As educators, whether parents or teachers, we have ample opportunities to forgive our charges! Remember that they are immature and need our grace. It is important that we do not hold on to resentments or label children negatively, even when their behaviour seems to merit it. When we forgive, we release our spirits from unforgiveness and resentment and also release those offending us to face God's dealings. While we hold on to negative judgement it maybe that we block God's work in them.

---

19 Matthew 18:21-22
20 NIV footnote to v.22

Justice

It is reckoned that teachers make an average of a thousand judgements/decisions every working day. Children have a strong sense of fair play—we need to be consistent and fair. To reflect God's character of just dealings and decisions we will need to ask for God's wisdom. The apostle James tells us that if we need wisdom we are to ask God who is willing to give it generously to all.[21] Just as God is not hasty in judgement so we need to be careful. I have often found that, where it is possible to do so, it is wise to sleep on decisions overnight. It is amazing how often God brings clarity, or even fresh evidence and perspective the following day.

The Life-Saver

Does all this sound an impossible challenge? The apostle Paul provides a 'life-saver' for us. He helps us understand we cannot possibly do what God requires in our own strength. Paul found the secret: he said, "For when I am weak then I am strong."[22] How could this be?

God showed him that, when he was weak, he could press into God's grace-power. "My grace is sufficient for you, for my power is made perfect in weakness."[23] Paul rejoiced in this revelation and said: "Therefore I will boast all the more gladly about my weaknesses … in insults, in hardships, in persecutions, in difficulties. For when I am weak, then I am strong."[24]

A new headmaster attended one of our training conferences. He listened attentively to our sessions and was very earnest. When we reached this challenge to let God's character be formed in us, these verses of Paul brought him sudden revelation and release. "I can't do it!" he exulted. "I can't do it! But God can do it through me!" He had laid hold of the life-saver! He went on to be a good headteacher, trusting in God's Spirit to help him in his weakness—as he helps us all! In the next chapter we explore how to cultivate the love of God in our classrooms.

---

21 James 1:5
22 2 Corinthians 12:10
23 2 Corinthians 12:9
24 2 Corinthians 12:9-11

Chapter Seven
The Kingdom of Love in the Classroom

The content of this chapter has been inspired by 'The Kingdom of Love and the Pride of Life' by Edward J. Carnell. I can honestly say this book has had a huge impact on me and I will be quoting from it frequently.

In education, as we have seen, we are commanded by Jesus to 'seek first the Kingdom of God and his righteousness'.[1] This guides us to educate, lead and run our schools in a way that pleases the King (Jesus) and works out the principles we find in his word. It is unfortunately true that the principles of the Kingdom can be applied vigorously and legalistically but without love. I have visited schools where this is sadly the case and it provokes the worst sort of rebellion in the pupils.

Carnell emphasises and expands the truth that God's Kingdom is about love. As we see in 1 John 4:8, God *is* love. This is his very nature. Therefore it can be seen that we are to be motivated and guided by love. Jesus placed the greatest importance on the two commandments to love God and our neighbour, saying that on these two depend all the rest.[2] The Apostle Paul's exhortation is 'do everything in love'.[3]

---

1 Matthew 6:33
2 Matthew 22:37-40
3 1 Corinthians 15:14

What Is Love?

Love is a very overworked and devalued word in the English language: I love my dog; I love chocolate; I love my wife; I love God. Jesus' repeated command was to love one another.[4] We badly need love redefined if we are to understand how properly to pursue the Kingdom of love in our schools.

Carnell defines love in this way: "Love is an act of unconditional acceptance. It receives another person just as he is, without one plea. It raises no legal barriers; it says, 'I accept you, you count.' Love is always kind and truthful, and it seeks nothing but kindness and truth in return."[5] Unconditional acceptance of others, which is non-judgemental or critical, is clearly foundational. We are to accept others because they, like us, are created in God's image or likeness and so are worthy of respect whatever their colour, creed, faith or non-faith.

The love that is of God is expressed by the Greek word *agape*. Agape means a love that gives regardless of return. We see it in the Apostle John's stark definition: 'this is how we know what love is; Jesus Christ laid down his life for us'.[6] Love may involve emotion but it is primarily an act of self-giving. It does not require a pay-back.

In 1 Corinthians 13, Paul gives us a beautiful and comprehensive list of the qualities of love. If you are an educator in any capacity, try it on for size and assess yourself according to the following list!

---

4   John 15:17
5   E.J. Carnell: The Kingdom of Love and the Pride of Life p.7
6   1 John 3:16

Love is	Love is not
Patient	Impatient
Kind	Unkind
Protective	Exposing
Trusting	Suspecting
Hopes	Doubtful
Perseveres	Faint hearted
Content	Envious
Modest	Boastful
Humble	Proud
Appropriately moral	Rude/coarse
Considerate of others	Self-seeking
Slow to anger	Easily angered/quick-tempered
Forgiving	Keeping a record of wrongs
Rejoices with truth/honesty	Delighting in evil

None of us is perfect—we need the 'life-saver'—and yet this gives us something to aim for with the help of the Holy Spirit.

How it Looks in the Flesh

There is no greater example of this sort of love than Jesus Christ himself on earth e.g. Love shown to all—even his judgements of the Pharisees was love bringing correction and discipline with the hope that they would change and catch God's heart.

In further examples we can see his love as inclusive acceptance without condemnation for prostitutes, tax-collectors and the thief on the cross.

We can see his love without partiality towards the rich young ruler, the children, and Nicodemus.

We can see his love as compassion and healing for the leper, the widow of Nain and the people who lacked a spiritual shepherd.

We can see his love as mercy towards the woman caught in adultery.

'Love implies a vital sharing of natures. It is a habit of life born of the convictions of the heart, which prompts a person to do as he would be done by. All people crave signs that they are needed and wanted. Love cheerfully gives these signs. Love does all it can to remove barriers to fellowship. It eases strained relations; it resists boasting and presence.... Since love has extraordinary powers of adaptability, it needs no handbook of morals to guide it. It simply adjusts its response to the situation. A gentle smile relieves the fear of censure; a pat on the back encourages manliness. Love is always appreciative; it listens or speaks when the moment is right, it is never patronising.'[7]

The First Duty of Love

Carnell depicts the first duty of love: 'to do as you would be done by'.[8] This is known as Jesus' 'golden rule'. He said: "So in everything do to others what you would have them do to you."[9] The golden rule can be found in earlier (3BC) Jewish writings but it is stated in a negative way: "What you hate, do to no one else." (Tobit: 4:15).[10] However, Jesus states it in a much more positive way.

Love is active not passive—it's what we *do*. Atticus Finch, the lawyer father, encouraged his children to do this in 'To Kill a Mocking Bird' when they struggled with their difficult neighbours. He said, "You never really understand a person until you consider things from his point of view ... until you climb into his skin and walk around in it."[11] Love tries to empathise with others and then expresses itself in acts of kindness. We are not capable of sustaining such love in our own strength. 'Love expresses itself in acts of benevolence, kindness and mercy in which heart, mind and will are united because they are motivated and

---

7   Carnell
8   Carnell: p.21
9   Matthew 7:12
10 David H. Stern: Jewish New Testament Commentary p.33
11 Harper Lee: To Kill a Mocking Bird p.30 (Warner Books, USA 1982)

empowered by God. Such love goes beyond what one can generate of oneself, because it has its origin in God'.[12]

Love as the Channel for Teaching

Love is a medium (or channel) of knowledge because love opens the heart of the learner to receive. 'Unless love opens the door to the heart access is denied.'[13] Many intellectuals refuse to accept this as a medium of knowledge. In the classroom love is conveyed mainly through the language we use. Proverbs says that the tongue can be 'a tree of life' i.e. 'up-building' or it can crush the Spirit.[14] I experienced the tongue, negatively, in my own schooling and many teachers I have spoken to in many countries have acknowledged their similar experiences with teachers. My maths teacher in the first year of grammar school when I was 11 years old was a sarcastic and cynical man. In my primary school I had loved Maths and came second in the class of about 30. But at the grammar school I was confused as there was no connection with the previous maths curriculum and neither did this teacher explain things more than once. I lost all confidence against his withering sarcasm. He favoured only the brightest pupils and ultimately put me along with about 10 others in a column of desks which he sneeringly addressed as: 'The Brains Trust'. My love for maths died and my hatred for him grew! At the end of that first year I was 32nd in a class of 34! This had a major detrimental effect on me and my ability to learn maths for five more years until a more humane teacher gave me understanding. In future years when I became a Christian, I realised this first teacher needed my forgiveness.

This illustrates a simple but profound principle in education. Unless your teacher accepts you and shows this 'love' through encouragement and help, learning is disadvantaged or, at worst, blocked. 'There is no level of life in which love fails to enlarge knowledge.'[15] God always intended learning to come through a living relationship with the teacher. The Russian psychologist, Lev Vygotsky, proved the importance of a positive relationship in the research he carried out as we will see

---

12   D. H. Stern: Jewish N.T. Commentary
13   E. J. Carnell: The Kingdom of Love and the Pride of Life p.47
14   Proverbs 15:4
15   E. J. Carnell: The Kingdom of Love and the Pride of Life p.46

in Chapter 9. He proved that a class which was taught only factual lessons with absolutely no encouragement, warmth or praise, learned less than a parallel class who received those qualities.

Every week The Times Educational Supplement carries an article about an adult's memory and gratitude for a relational teacher from their childhood who spurred them on and won their devotion. It is an interesting fact that, after I had forgiven this maths teacher, my love for maths returned! Many adults (teachers and parents among them) have recognised that they disliked or loved a subject because of the personality and the quality of relationship with the teacher.

When challenged to love in the way we have described, the harassed teacher may be saying 'This is all very well—but you don't teach *my* class!' The truth is that it is hard to love all our pupils and, as none of us are perfect, we will not find it easy to maintain a loving approach throughout the varied experiences of the day, which sometimes includes irate parents! When he was on earth, Jesus needed to renew his strength by time with his Father just as we do. This love is the key to all learning and it *is* possible to love all our students by the enabling power of the Holy Spirit; even, or perhaps more especially, God will give us grace to love the most difficult and, if we will ask him, the keys to connecting with that sort of student because God loves them. If we will ask, we will receive.[16]

Where Do We Begin?

Love begins in the heart and it is mainly expressed through kindness. The first act of kindness is to show each child that you accept them as a person, regardless of their ability. This meets a foundational human need. Kindness is further expressed when we show grace for pupils' imperfections and their failures to fulfil requirements or expectations—even in mundane but important matters, such as looking after their own property, or that of the school. However, Kingdom love is not a soft option: it is loving to correct and to discipline. It is an atmosphere we set and promote by treating our pupils as we would like to be treated.

---

16 Luke 11:9-13

Love as Corrective Discipline

The Bible makes it clear that correction is part of loving in the process of bringing our children to maturity. It may involve loss of privilege or punishment of some kind as a consequence of wrong choices. 'No discipline is pleasant at the time, but painful. Later on, however, it produces a harvest of righteousness and peace for those who have been trained by it.'[17] Whilst correction is needed, it must be redemptive and motivated by a love which has vision for the pupil's potential character formation and gives them strategies and hope for change. More on 'Wisdom in Discipline' will be found in Chapter 11.

Teacher as Priest: Wear the Mantle of Weakness!

Don't get freaked out by the religious term 'priest': just read on! As teachers we need to remember what it was like to be a pupil. We were in their 'shoes' once. Can we remember? My own experience of the cynical and tyrannical maths teacher I described meant that I was a more sympathetic teacher of maths because I knew what it was like to struggle with understanding or to need a second explanation.

Jesus put on a mantle of weakness by becoming a human being like us. He experienced what it was like to be us. He was tempted in every way as we are![18] His role was that of a priest who represents us like an intermediary 'go-between'. He brings us before God in prayer and from God gives blessings back to us. Another aspect of love in action is that we intercede for them, as Christ our great High Priest does for us.[19]

'He is able to deal gently with those who are ignorant (*untaught*) and are going astray since he is subject to weakness'[20] — the italics in brackets are mine. In the same way, we need to deal gently, although sometimes firmly, with weakness in our pupils. This sort of understanding approach will often unlock a positive response in them. In addition, this can model to our pupils how to handle weakness when we fail.

---

17 Hebrews 12:11
18 Hebrews 4:15
19 Hebrews 7:25
20 Hebrews 5:2

Unless You Become as Children …

When Jesus said that unless we change and become like little children we cannot enter the Kingdom of God,[21] he clearly did not mean that we revert to childishness. Carnell believes that happy children operate from what he calls 'the convictions of the heart' and that (unless they have been abused) they will naturally love. 'Happy children are so full of love that they extend their overtures of fellowship in every direction. They talk to their toys, they sing to their pets. The whole world is a kingdom of love.'[22]

This love derives from innate convictions understood by children. They also learn this love from stories, for example that good must triumph over evil in the end or that a good, kind person may be hard done by, as in the story of Cinderella, but that the story will end happily for her. 'Whether the intellect will own it or not, the heart has its convictions. These convictions say that a person is good when he is kind and truthful and that in the end a good person has nothing to fear. The first part clarifies love, while the second part clarifies hope. To love is to be kind and truthful; to hope is to believe that things will work out happily in the end. The issue is as simple as that.'[23]

As we mature and leave childhood behind, the pressures and demands of earning a living can quench the heart's convictions and make us too busy to love others. If our hearts then become hardened, it is only too easy to live only by intellect and self-effort. Yet a childlike trust in a benevolent heavenly Father is at the heart of the nature of adult faith.

Without Love We Have Nothing

We may be a very gifted person with great knowledge, but without love it counts for nothing in God's Kingdom.[24] We may be a highly qualified person, but without love we cannot teach the way God requires. The love present in a school is intangible but it can be felt and it comes from the head and staff. It is all too

---

21 Matthew 18:3
22 E. J. Carnell: The Kingdom of Love and The Pride of Life p.17
23 *Ibid.* p.17
24 1 Corinthians 13:1-2

easy to lose the spirit of love in a school. Recently, I learned of a school where the head, a father figure, left the school too much in the hands of a competent administrator. Within a few months, parents and children were uneasy and some began to leave. Love had gone from the school. The head realised he must return, sow his vision again in the teachers and, most importantly, demonstrate the love of God to all so that the school family can be revived.

We may have the most state-of-the-art building and equipment but without love it is an empty shell! As we pursue the Kingdom in education, let us remember that it is all about love and without this our work counts for nothing. Perhaps the last word should come from the apostle Paul who sums it up by saying, "The entire law is summed up in a single command: 'Love your neighbour as yourself.'"[25]

---

25 Galations 5:14

Chapter Eight
Every One a Gem

I praise you because I am fearfully and wonderfully made. (Psalm 139:14)

I've been in many primary schools all over the world and seen children grouped according to animals, colours and film characters but the most appropriate of all was where the children were grouped as precious gems: Diamonds, Emeralds, Rubies, Sapphires. For this is what they are.

I vividly remember the summer morning when I held my own first gem: our newly-born baby daughter in my arms. I was filled with wonder at the perfection of this tiny bundle; right down to her little toe-nail everything was in place although, as yet, minute. Her fingers were very long and as I gazed at them, I began to wonder: what will she be like? Are these fingers the sign of artistic gifting? Will she be a pianist? My daughter is very gifted and, over 40 years later, is now married to a wonderful man and much of her destiny is being revealed. Yes, she was to be artistic; her drawings and paintings bring delight to us all. Her love and affinity with animals is surely a gift; as for the pianist, there aren't any signs of that talent, although there is still time!

We are born with our personality and gifting, our physical features and physique already wonderfully determined by God's plan. The code is genetically in place through our DNA. A friend of ours once wittily redefined this term as 'Divine Nature Attributes'! How true. It is not only physical and emotional attributes that are potentially present but our spiritual potential in Christ as we are made in His divine image. The baby fills us with a sense of awe because, although we can now see a physical being, the mystery of his or her future destiny in the larger world is still to be revealed. The key to that child finding their true destiny will depend on them finding Jesus Christ as their personal Lord and Saviour.

God leaves us in no doubt that children are important and valuable to Him. As a Father, God loves and wants to nurture and protect the children He creates. As well as telling us that we are 'fearfully and wonderfully made', Psalm 139 declares that he created us in our 'inmost being' i.e. our personality and character, in our mother's womb. His eyes saw our unformed body as an embryo.

God's Call to Jeremiah

The young Jeremiah's conversation with God reveals more stunning truths regarding the time before birth:

God: 'Before I formed you in the womb, I knew you. Before you were born, I set you apart; I appointed you as a prophet to the nations.'

Jeremiah: 'Ah Sovereign Lord', I said, 'I do not know how to speak. I am only a child.'

God: 'Do not say, "I am only a child." You must go to everyone I send you to and say whatever I command you. Do not be afraid of them, for I am with you and will rescue you,' declares the Lord[1]

This record of Jeremiah's calling from God when he was clearly still young, tells us two amazing facts. The first is that God reveals that he 'knew' him *before* he formed Jeremiah—prior to conception! The word 'knew', as used in Hebrew, represents intimate knowledge. In other words, God 'knew' Jeremiah, probably in the sense that he had him in his mind as a unique creation. God's priority is that all of his children are made for relationship with him. The second fact is that God has a purpose for Jeremiah. He has designed him with the right personality

---

1   Jeremiah 1:5-6

to be both tender-hearted (Jeremiah is going to grieve over the unfaithfulness of God's people Israel) and full of perseverance, for he will endure much opposition from his people in order to be faithful to what God will show him. It is my conviction that the revelation that we are known before conception and also created with God's purpose for us in mind can be applied to all of us as God's children. I also believe, although it cannot be proved, that every illegitimate child is also designed and known by the Lord. In that sense there are no 'accidents'. This indicates that we are all called to fulfil a purpose God has planned for us before we were born. Sadly, unless we are born again, we are unable to fully enter into God's chosen destiny for us although, we may by his providence, end up in the right profession. Every child is created uniquely to know God and to fulfil the purpose for which he or she is uniquely designed. It may be to teach, to nurse, to direct business, to be an engineer, an artist, a builder, a politician, a pastor or an economist—the possible callings of God are varied indeed!

Endless Variety

Every child, as I am sure all parents will agree, is uniquely different even if they are identical triplets or twins! It never ceases to amaze me how different children from the same parents can be. Our own three children were all completely different and unique personalities. Two of my grandchildren from our youngest daughter and her husband are boys. One is studious and always hungry for more knowledge, while the other is always inventing models using every cardboard box he can get his hands on! Our son has twin girls and again they show striking differences in character and interests—even in their food preferences! At just a few months old one instinctively loved apple; the other, just as instinctively, wouldn't touch it! One of them is always a pioneering and daring leader; the other is intuitive, a day-dreamer and graceful dancer. Yet both shared the same womb at the same time! God loves creating endless variety!

Created and Equipped for Purpose

God has prepared 'good works' for us. Paul, the apostle, writes that we are 'God's workmanship, created in Christ Jesus to do good works, which God prepared in advance for us to do'.[2] Now whom God calls, he also prepares for that purpose in personality, aptitude and skills (some of which are genetically transferred and some learned). It is a joy to see many of our pupils finding God's purpose for their lives. Many are in the UK but many are also serving in distinctly Christian ways in a variety of countries.

Gifts for Purpose

God has given each of us gifts which, I believe, go with the good works (our calling) which God has prepared for us. In our pupils we can begin to see clues to their gifting and calling by the things they do. In Romans 12 we read of a selection of giftings according to the grace God has given us. Some of us have several giftings—most of us have more than one. The gifts listed are: prophecy, serving, teaching, encouraging, contributing to the needs of others and leading. I do not think this is an exhaustive list. God creates a huge variety: some are linked to a career; administration, entrepreneurial, artistic creativity, mathematical, linguistic or scientific skills; or practical vocational skills, such as carpentry, metal-working. The list is endless. We see these demonstrated in many biblical characters. Nehemiah had organisational skills to oversee a major project like re-building Jerusalem's walls; Noah, although a farmer, oversaw a huge carpentry project; Deborah was a feisty activist and prophetic communicator who also had the boldness to be a war leader! David had the gift of governing with justice; Joseph in the Old Testament had entrepreneurial strategy and servanthood; Daniel had administrative wisdom; Bezalel and Oholiab, mentioned in Exodus [3], had craft and design skills; the apostle Paul was a logical and gifted theologian—and so on. Each of these was equipped with the gifts needed for the job God called them to do.

In Ephesians Chapter 4, Paul tells us of gifts given by Christ to help build his church. Here we find some are called to be apostles, prophets, pastors, teachers and evangelists. Again it is possible to have more than one of these abilities but usually we are motivated strongly in one area. In children the teacher may find a

---

2   Ephesians 2:10
3   Exodus 31:1-11

budding apostle who challenges the way things are done and provides an alternative overview. The budding prophet may be very wordy, given to moods and towards rather 'black and white' opinions and may not be good at administration. The pastor will usually have many friends because his caring nature draws them to him. The teacher may be bossy and not good at putting up with more visionary characters or unstructured situations.

Children are immature and so we may see negative aspects of gifting as well as positive clues. For example, a budding administrator dislikes change and disorder but has to learn flexibility. A potential leader can often be a handful in the classroom; they may be bossy or arrogant and they often challenge the teacher! They have to learn servanthood. A pupil with an evangelist gifting has to learn the discipline of gaining academic skills, although he or she longs to be outside the confines of school, mixing with others.

The Holy Spirit also distributes gifts as listed in 1 Corinthians 12. These gifts are usually for the work of the church in outreach; gifts such as word of knowledge, healing, and miracles, although they may also function in church meetings. The word of wisdom is a gift we all need on occasions, but some exercise it more regularly.

Gems need setting firmly in the right place. One preacher said: "A loose gem in a setting is easily lost." God wants us to pray and plan for our children's future that they may be born again and helped to find their place in God's plan. It is good to encourage parents to pray about the destiny of their children and to observe the clues in them. Clues can also be gained from favourite bible characters who they wish to emulate or favourite books of the bible. Where prophetic words are given, these can envision us to see how God sees our children.

The Opponent of Our Destiny

There is an enemy, Satan, who seeks to discourage and even destroy our children. Children from difficult home situations, adopted or orphan children, may have experienced pain, rejection or trauma. These will lock up their gifting. Time and patient, loving care or prayer will be needed to unlock the heart and free the gifting to develop. We see that Moses had a major struggle with fear at having to face the Egyptian court where he had been guilty of murder as a young man. Yet his gifting was to lead and to communicate. God had to encourage him with the support of his brother Aaron until he grew in confidence. Gideon was afflicted with inferiority as well as fear—yet he had the potential to be a national leader. Joseph's future was blotted out for many years by his brothers' jealousy and hatred. Doubtless he seemed arrogant and was unwise yet he suffered much pain and injustice. God is able to use the painful experiences to shape our characters. Forgiveness is the huge key for unlocking us and our gifting from the pain of the past.

On occasion, the enemy sets an opponent against us to destroy us. David's heart was open and his desire was to serve and please King Saul. Yet the enemy incited Saul to jealous hatred and he even attempted to murder David. God delivered him from this fate and shaped this gem for leadership. A young lady I met in our church responded to my teaching on Christian education. She had trained as a teacher but her confidence was so shattered by a bullying headteacher that she left the profession. Through prayer, she forgave this man and the lie that she had believed about her inability. The result was she became one of the most gifted teachers in a Christian school—the gem was replaced in its right setting.

Made in God's Image

Each child is made 'in his image', even as Adam and Eve were. What does this mean? Wayne Grudem in his book 'Systematic Theology'[4] explains the phrase used in Genesis where God says: "Let us make man in our image after our likeness."[5] (note that 'man' is used as a generic term for 'mankind' not just for the male sex). He gives this definition: *'The fact that man is in the image of God means that man is like God and represents him.'*[6] Grudem explains that the Hebrew word used for 'image' is *tselem* which means similar but not identical.

---

4   For a full explanation of the ways in which we are made in God's image, see Wayne Grudem: Systematic Theology p.442-450
5   Genesis 1:26
6   Wayne Grudem: Systematic Theology p.442

As each child reflects a likeness of the Creator, so each requires our respect and acceptance of his design. It is very important for teachers to accept and value every child in their care. Whether or not they are good students, they are divinely designed. All are different yet all have the same needs: to be accepted, affirmed and loved. All are different yet all are designed to be born again of God's Spirit, to know Him and to be filled with His Spirit. Paul, writing to the Corinthians, tells us our bodies are created to be 'temples'—places of worship where God's Spirit can dwell.[7]

The Image Was Marred

Whilst created in his image, that image, as we saw in Adam and Eve's story, was marred by sin which we have inherited from our ancestors. No matter how committed to God their parents may be, children still need to face and realise their own need of a saviour. My experience over many years is that children know when they are ready to respond personally to the message of the Gospel. Rather, perhaps we should say, God draws them to himself at the right time. In assemblies where I would share the story of why Jesus died, I would not labour or try to force response but saw that some children responded quickly when it was the right time and others hesitated and maybe had a little struggle, but on a subsequent occasion, may well respond clearly. Without exception, whenever I led children in a prayer to give Jesus control of their lives, they always said they felt joyful and peaceful. No wonder! They had been set free from the reign of sin and death inherited from their ancestors, to the joyful reign of Jesus as King and the releasing law of the Spirit of Life.[8]

Made to Praise Him

Once born again, the Holy Spirit in them wants to express praise to God through their personality and gifting. So some will excel in playing instruments, some will excel in singing, some in dance or drama and some in all of them! Children are created to give praise to God and to hear from Him. One of the most important

---

7   1 Corinthians 3:16
8   Romans 8:2

things we can train children to do is to give praise and also to learn to be quiet before him, allowing him to impress his thoughts in them. He does this in many ways but, most frequently, as they learn to wait expectantly, God gives children simple pictures.

Growing in Hearing from God

Even children as young as five or six can 'see' such pictures and grow to interpret them. It's been my privilege to experience this with children in Europe, Canada, Africa and India. Often the Holy Spirit teaches them through contrast: for instance, a healthy flower in a vase of water and a wilting flower in an empty vase. They learn to ask God for the meaning and, most often, God is impressing on them their ability to choose, whether to keep 'drinking' from God or to become weak. The Old Testament prophet, Joel, promised: "Your sons and daughters will prophesy."[9]

These simple pictures are the beginnings of children learning to 'prophesy', i.e. to listen and give out messages from God, just as Jeremiah did when God schooled him with pictures of an almond tree branch or a boiling pot.[10] Many of our children have matured in this and frequently pray and prophesy over visitors. On several occasions a simple word has been remarkably confirmed. One leader of a Bible college in India was doubting a word given to him in Yonggi Cho's large church in South Korea. When he visited our school in England, a boy gave him the exact same message: he was to 'expand and build'. He, and we, were amazed!

Receiving God's word can be amusing and appropriate at the same time. When I was head and also had responsibility for a class, one of my boy pupils (Dan — not his real name), was somewhat disturbed and caused me quite a lot of trouble. One day he even ran out of school with me having to chase him! Soon after this, we were asking God to speak to us individually and ran out of time to hear the responses. I suggested that these children write on a piece of paper any word that they felt was from God and leave it on the desk for me to see later. When I

---

9 Joel 2:28
10 Jeremiah 1:11, 13

saw 9-year old Dan's word, it was a biblical reference to an obscure verse in the book of Job which said 'Bear with me a little longer'! This became even more confirmed when, a couple of months later, his family moved to another area to live and he had to leave our school!

Destiny: Fellowship and Function

Our privilege as teachers and parents is to prepare our children for the 'good works' God has prepared for them to do. This will involve masses of encouragement but also correction. As we saw in Chapter 7, God's intention is that our children are to be discipled in a relationship of unconditional love. This discipleship will involve teaching, encouragement and correction. The most unhappy child is the child who is never corrected. Without correction and boundaries there is no security. The most famous passage on training and love is in Hebrews 12:5-6 which we will examine further in Chapter 11. In this passage it is clear that true love involves loving correction.

When God looks at children he sees their whole lives from beginning to end, whereas we only see the child as he is through our own short-sightedness. We need to beware of limiting or wrongly labelling a pupil. They are his creation and he has plans for them. As we saw earlier, the experience of Jeremiah is significant for us. As a young person, possibly in his teens or even younger, Jeremiah has an encounter with the Lord which revealed the plan for his life.

Shaping the Gems

All gems need shaping and polishing. Living together in the class and wider school community, our children rub up against one another's different characters and although this can cause friction it also trains our children in tolerance of others. They learn to appreciate every pupil who is created in the image of God and for whom God has specific plans and destiny. One of the most up-building activities is to ask a group of pupils to take it in turns in focusing on one person at a time and every other in the group speaks only positive aspects and qualities they see in that person. This is a great encouragement to each individual, building self-esteem, and counteracts our pupils' tendency to see only negatives or to be cynical and sarcastic. In addition to shaping, precious gems also need correction and pruning—more about this will be addressed in Chapter 11.

The High Priest in the Old Testament wore a breastplate on which precious stones representing each of the twelve tribes were placed. As he went into the Lord's presence he carried their names over his heart and represented them before God. This is a principle of the priestly role of the teacher bringing their pupils before God in prayer. As we value each pupil God will enable us to relate to them and teach them with greater success.

When we are released to operate in our gifting, we experience joy and fulfilment. Eric Liddell, the hero depicted in the film 'Chariots of Fire' faced opposition from his family regarding his athletics. He persevered and said simply: "I feel God's pleasure when I run". Pleasure and fulfilment in our career are sure signs that we are operating in our gifting. God wants us to enjoy serving him! Our task as teachers requires much skill. In the next chapter we will learn from a Master teacher.

CHAPTER NINE
The Diamond Creator

Jesus is recognised world-wide as an excellent teacher. He left no written record but invested himself in his class of 12 disciples, some of whom recorded his life and teaching. What made Jesus such a successful teacher? Of course, he was the Son of God and he therefore, perfectly embodied the truth he was teaching, unsullied by sin. As we consider him, there are several factors which made him so effective, many of these we can also employ.

Integrity Gives Us Authority

In Jewish education, 'The aim of the Jewish teacher was not so much to develop certain intellectual or practical faculties in his disciple but rather to summon his learner to submit to the authority of the divine message of the Scripture upon which he was commenting. Here the Jew's whole personality is involved: to be taught called for radical obedience to that higher divine reality outside oneself.'[1]

Jesus modelled this and more. He spoke with integrity and authority. He <u>was</u> what he taught. His were not merely cerebral concepts but he modelled his teaching by his life style. He could challenge his hearers to trust their heavenly Father for provision because he himself practised this daily as an itinerant teacher. When he spoke it was with authority. 'When Jesus had finished saying these things the

---
1 Marvin R. Wilson: Our Father Abraham p.291

crowds were amazed at his teaching because he taught as one who had authority and not as their teachers of the law.'[2] The Jewish teachers evidently were hypocritical, challenging people to give to God when they themselves did not. Jesus exposed this in a scathing judgement in Matthew's gospel, Chapter 23. Jesus' authority came from the fact that he was speaking out of integrity and example. This is important for us to recognise and embrace in our teaching.

Partnership with the Holy Spirit

Jesus was so effective because he was filled with and worked with the Holy Spirit. It is interesting to note that Jesus never uttered one public word of teaching until he was baptised and had received the Holy Spirit. From then on he worked in perfect partnership with the Spirit, relying on the Father's guidance through him. He frequently says that his teaching is not his own but what the Father gives him to say. "My teaching is not my own. It comes from him who sent me."[3] He also said that he could do nothing by himself but only what Father showed him to do.[4]

Dependent or Independent Teachers?

What does this mean for us who are imperfect teachers—how do we apply this? Jesus shows us how to be dependent, rather than independent, teachers. We are to ask God to help us by his Holy Spirit in planning lessons and in delivering them. It is very tempting for us to rely wholly on textbooks, syllabi or our own minds. So often we ignore the submission of our work to the Lord and remain 'wise in our own eyes',[5] i.e. limited to our own perspective. His Spirit is creative and a Spirit of wisdom who wishes to guide us into all truth.[6] He has keys to unlock our pupils; and inventive and imaginative ideas to make our lessons sparkle with life and fun. He also is able to reveal to us how to cause our teaching to reflect God and his wisdom. More about how this can work practically will be

---

2   Matthew 7:28-29
3   John 7:16
4   John 5:19-20
5   Proverbs 3:7
6   John 16:13

discovered in the next chapter.

I have experienced the promptings of the Spirit completely changing my plans. I was planning a junior term project on 'Space'. I had many ideas: we could study the Solar System and man's race to the moon: the structure of space rockets and lunar modules etc. Fortunately, I decided to stop and ask the Lord for his ideas. He instantly changed my perspective by saying: "Space is man's word for it but it's not empty; it's full—it's my universe." He then showed me how to talk about the beginning of the universe when he created it, and the end of it when Jesus returns to create a new heaven and new earth. We still used the ideas I had but the focus was changed. Instead of man conquering space, it became 'man exploring God's universe'. It was one of the best projects I have done and all because of a quick prayer and some listening.

How Do You Relate?

Another key factor that made Jesus so effective as a teacher was his relational ability. He did not speak above his audiences; he evidently welcomed them and cared about them, whatever their status. This meant that the warmth of Father's acceptance and love came from him and drew them. Unconditional love, as we have already said, is the key to all learning. If pupils get the impression that you don't like them, or that they are somehow unacceptable, their heart closes to your teaching.

Even Russian psychologist Lev Vygotsky[7], who was Jewish but apparently not a Christian, discovered the power of relational teaching. His research led him to teach two parallel classes the same lesson content over several weeks. With one class he was unemotional and gave no encouragement or warmth. To the other he was the opposite, building an affirming relationship. When he tested the knowledge and understanding of the two classes, he discovered that his relational approach increased the amount of learning. He called this the 'zpd' factor (zone of proximal development).

For him this proved that relational teaching was more effective and could lead a

---

7   Lev Vygotsky: Educational Psychology, written in 1926, translated and published in 1992.

pupil further in knowledge and understanding. Vygotsky also encouraged pupils' peer partnerships in learning as an effective motivator.

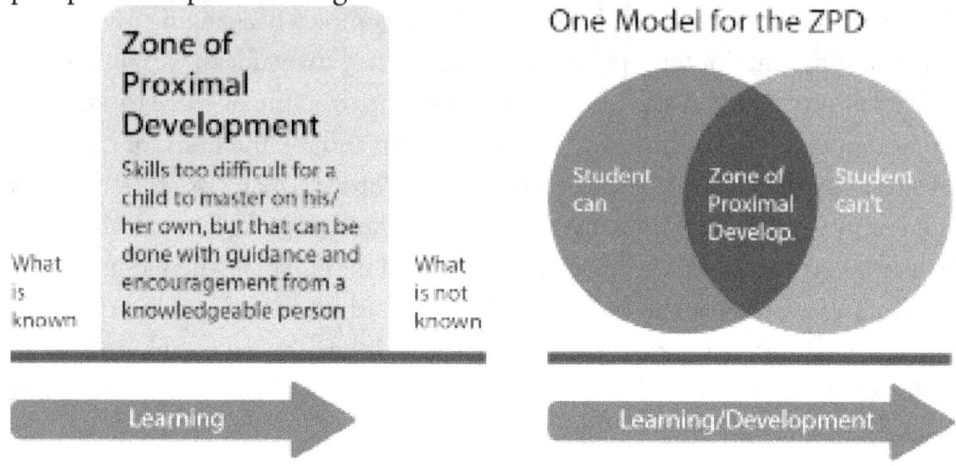

Study the Master

A study of Jesus' teaching approaches in the four gospels is well worth the effort to examine the way Jesus taught. This requires us to read the examples of Jesus' teaching with the eye of a teacher, rather than reading devotionally. We need to ask the questions: "Who is he teaching? What skills is he using? What are his main teaching points? How does he apply them?"

Jesus taught at least four different types of pupil. First, of course, he taught his disciples. Secondly, he taught the crowds. Thirdly, he taught the Jewish teachers of the Law, Pharisees and Sadducees. Fourthly, he dialogued with individuals. Each type of teaching was different. When teaching the disciples he would speak more directly and obviously encouraged their questions to ensure their understanding. He also taught them through challenging situations, as when there was no food to feed the crowds, and he said to them: "You give them something to eat."[8] When teaching the crowds he would use stories and agricultural analogies and, surprisingly, often did not explain stories. One example of this is the teaching of the Parable of the Weeds which he told simply as a story to the crowds

---

8   Mark 6:37

with no explanation[9]. Once they were in a house with Jesus, the disciples asked many questions so that Jesus fully explained the meaning to them. Frequently, we discover, the disciples were slow learners. "Do you still not understand?" he would ask. In one way this is encouraging for us—even the Master Teacher had pupils slow to grasp his teaching!

How to Handle the Difficult Pupils

Jesus' approach in teaching the Jewish leaders and 'experts of the law' was very different. They were usually opposing him and seeking to find fault. Frequently he would answer their question with another question. When they challenged him "Who gave you this authority?" he replied without answering directly: "I will also ask you a question. If you answer me I will tell you by what authority I am doing these things. John's baptism—where did it come from? Was it from heaven, or from men?"[10] This question completely disabled them, because they had not received John's baptism. They were afraid of losing the people's support because the people had accepted John. Another example is found in Matthew 15:1-7 where Jesus again challenges the Pharisees and teachers of the law regarding their hypocrisy. This might be an approach to use with pupils who challenge or oppose you! In addition he based his teaching and dialogue with them on the Mosaic Law (the Torah) which they purported to know and which they claimed as their authority. He would approach their questions logically, often asking: "What does the law of Moses say?"

After examining the Torah's words, Jesus would re-interpret them to reveal God's grace which was coming through him, who is described as 'full of grace and truth'.[11] There was frequent conflict over their legalistic rules which restricted the Sabbath and consequently prevented them from rejoicing for the healing of the sick; as when the man with the withered hand was healed by Jesus on the Sabbath.[12] Here his logical questioning revealed that they would help a trapped animal but not a human being!

---

9   Matthew 13:34-43
10 Matthew 21:24-25
11 John 1:14
12 Matthew 12:9-14

Jesus' teaching of individuals is best illustrated in the story of the Pharisee, Nicodemus, who came to him secretly at night. Using analogies of the wind and of birth, Jesus challenged and chided him, teaching him to see the need to be born again by the activity of the Holy Spirit.[13]

Other Skills of Jesus

Story

When we ask ourselves what methods and skills is he using in his teaching, we discover many 'tools' in his toolkit. Jesus' favourite method is to use a parable which could be either a brief or a long story. Stories engage the imagination and are easier to remember than a list of facts or principles. Jesus could have said: "I want to teach you about Father's unconditional love". Instead, he told the moving story of the Prodigal Son.[14] In the way he addressed his father he was actually saying: "I wish you were dead. I want my money now." Despite his rebellion and subsequent profligacy the Father welcomes and forgives his son, reflecting Father God's love. This story remains powerful and memorable in all cultures, depicting an analogy of Father God's patient and forgiving love.

Parables could also be brief, as in "The Kingdom of Heaven is like yeast that a woman took and mixed into a large amount of flour until it worked all through the dough".[15] Only 26 words! A parable is like a chocolate with a nut inside it. The story is the tasty chocolate but central to the story is one solid kingdom principle: the nut. In this case, it is that the kingdom permeates and changes everything like the yeast.

Logic

After delivering a man from a demon, Jesus answers an accusation that he is being used by the devil. Jesus uses the analogy of a strong man being overcome by a more powerful man.[16] Jesus is breaking the devil's power so how, logically,

---

13 John 3
14 Luke 15
15 Matthew 13:33
16 Luke 11:14-22

can Satan be casting Satan out of people's lives? For other examples see Matthew 15:1-9 and John 8:39-41.

Creative use of questions

Every teacher uses questions. Why is this effective? The question opens the heart of the learner. When he is about to teach about the kingdom, Jesus poses a question: "To what shall I compare the kingdom?"[17] This provokes the mind to be engaged and opens the heart to want to be given the correct answer. Such questions are especially useful when starting a new theme.

Jesus used rhetorical questions: "Why do you call me Lord, Lord and do not do what I say?"[18] He also used trick questions: "Is it lawful to heal on the Sabbath or not?"[19] Frequently Jesus ended a parable with the key question engaging the listener's response. After the parable of the Good Samaritan, which he told in answer to a listener's question, Jesus pushes the point home with the question: "Which of these three do you think was a neighbour to the man who fell into the hands of robbers?"[20]

Punchy punch lines!

Skill in punch lines, which succinctly capture the teaching principle, is another of Jesus' skills. Note that these often come at the end of the story. Did Jesus know, what psychologists now tell us, that the last thing taught is most easily remembered? Jesus' teaching on greed for money ends with the punch line: "For where your treasure is there will your heart be also."[21] His teaching on spiritual vision uses the simple analogy of the eye and light. It ends with the chilling conclusion: "If the light within you is darkness, how great is that darkness!"[22]

As teachers, we need to carefully consider where we set the main principle in the lesson. If not at the end, it needs to be repeated at the end. The punchier we can make it, the more memorable it will be. I once had this backfire on me when

---

17 Mark 4:30
18 Luke 4:46
19 Luke 14:3
20 Luke 10:36
21 Matthew 6:21
22 Matthew 6:23

in an assembly teaching I used the phrase: "Being proud is not allowed." This caught on, partly because it rhymed. At the end of term, after a production to the parents, I was praising the children and said: "I'm proud of you." With one voice they shot back: "Being proud is not allowed!"

Imagery and metaphor

Jesus used picture language all the time. He talked about himself in picture language: the Vine, the Shepherd, the Door, the Living Water, the Light of the World and many more. His imagery in the parables he told are vivid and relevant to the lives of the people he taught, who were mostly an agricultural people. Therefore, he used agricultural imagery and metaphor: the seed, the sower, the fruit tree, the field. The metaphor of spiritual riches is one of treasure which is sustained throughout with the striking imagery of thieves, moths, rust added to it.[23] It is worth considering the type of imagery which will relate to modern pupils: in this digital age, graphic computer and technology images and the use of YouTube should probably feature strongly! We need to find relevant imagery and metaphor that can connect with our pupils' lifestyles and setting—whether urban or rural.

Bridging—teaching from the known to the unknown

This should be the practice of every good teacher. First, we must know our pupils and their prior knowledge. Then we 'bridge' by leading them in consecutive steps of learning to the new knowledge we wish them to experience. Jesus practised this on several occasions. "You have heard that it was said: 'An eye for an eye'; 'Love your neighbour and hate your enemy'. But I tell you: Love your enemies and pray for those who persecute you, that you may be sons of your Father in heaven."[24] When calling his first disciples, Jesus did not say to Simon Peter and Andrew: "Follow me; I will give you a three-year course on evangelism." He knew they were fishermen so he bridged, using language they would understand: "Come, follow me and I will make you fishers of men."[25] Again, to the woman at the well—Jesus could have said: "You are an immoral woman. I can be your Saviour." Instead he bridged using water, which was the setting and what she had

---

23 Matthew 6:19-21
24 Matthew 5:43
25 Matthew 4:19

come to gather: "If you knew the gift of God and who it is that asks you for a drink, you would have asked him and he would have given you living water."[26]

Responding to a student's initiative
This, of course, needs discernment as some students are experts at trying to lead us off course! Often we dislike interruption to our lesson flow. Jesus was in the middle of a teaching inside a crowded house when he was interrupted by the roof tiles falling in! Undeterred, Jesus was quick to discern the situation and to recognise the students' initiative and faith on behalf of their paralysed friend! A miracle followed. Jesus' prepared lesson is presumably abandoned or at least delayed!

As teachers, we need to allow for student's questions and initiative which may sometimes surprise us or catch us off guard. Ideally, learning is a creative, interactive partnership. The Holy Spirit can prompt ideas and questions from our pupils as long as we make room for this and encourage it. This requires flexibility. It also requires us not to be too hasty in dismissing pupil initiatives or questions.

Demonstration
This hardly needs mentioning as all teachers will know the power of demonstration and visual aids. Interactive white boards have immeasurably opened up creative possibilities for us. Research on the brain, which still remains a mystery, implies that some pupils learn by facts and lists (a left hemisphere function) but others especially need to have pictures and diagrams as they use their right hemisphere more dominantly. This hemisphere recognises pictures and images. Jesus, of course, used demonstration mostly in healing and deliverance, which revealed the coming of his kingdom in power to set free those who were oppressed through illness or demonic forces. In addition, Jesus used every-day visual aids teaching, for example, how to combat worry by the example of his provision for birds and flowers.[27]

The voice
We cannot know the sound of Jesus' voice in these teachings but it must have been attractive, clear and authoritative. The voice is the teacher's prime tool. It

---
26 John 4:10
27 Matthew 6:25-30

needs to be well-paced, varied in tone and at the right volume. Some classes are burdened by teachers who shout at them all day. Others endure monotonous, lifeless voices. When I was in my first teaching practice as a student, my mentor teacher nailed me over my voice which she said lacked authority and was too easy-going. This was the best correction I ever had. Ask a colleague to hear you teach to get a more accurate assessment on your voice.

Review

The practice of review, i.e. summarising and re-visiting your main points, is a key to impressing the learning in your pupils' memories. It takes 10-15 minutes but is invaluable in discovering whether your pupils have really understood your teaching. The deception about teaching is that we may feel, because we have taught at length and demonstrated, it is now fully understood. Through summarising, by questioning or pair review, we can greatly enhance learning. It is suggested that this stores knowledge in long-term memory through revisiting the material and re-articulating it.

By studying Jesus the teacher and applying his skills, we can become far better teachers—let's do it!

Chapter Ten
Mining for Diamonds

If our aim in education is wisdom, we must face the challenge of discovering how to mine the diamonds of the Word of God for our curriculum. God's word, says the Psalmist, makes wise even the simple.[1] To teach a curriculum without God's word is to deprive our children of wisdom and life. Moses said to the people of Israel, as he released the commandments of God before he died: "They are not just idle words for you—they are your life."[2]

Tyrants through the ages have suppressed the word of God. Communism banned it and ultimately collapsed. In the reign of Louis XIV of France, Christian schools were destroyed by him. He said: "Teachers you can teach but without the Bible."[3] The enemy of our souls knows its power."

The words of God are not like any other words: they have an inherent dynamic. "The word of God is living and active. Sharper than any double-edged sword", says the writer to the Hebrews.[4] God's word is full of power and life because it is pure truth. Furthermore, not only does it penetrate to the inner heart, but it is a 'doing' agent that goes on working and it *will* produce results. God promises through the prophet Isaiah that his word will not return to him empty, but will

---

1   Psalm 19
2   Deuteronomy 32:47
3   Notes from a Lecture: 'Christian Education: An Historical Perspective' by Luc Bussiere given in France in 2008
4   Hebrews 4:12

yield fruit. As teachers we need to regain our faith in the power of the word of God as we sow it into our pupils' lives.

Our schools need to make time to study, meditate and memorise the Bible. I was deeply impacted through a visit to a Jewish school when I learned that they spend 40-80% (in varied schools) of their timetable simply studying, discussing and learning the Torah. One Rabbi responded to my astonishment and questions about academic subjects by assuring me that their students passed well in exams because there were insights to all the subjects in their scriptures. Are we giving enough priority time to God's Word?

Stored in the Memory

Scripture memory has power. Muslims also teach their children a verse a day from the Qu' Aran beginning at the age of three. Our older pupils learned a passage of the Bible each week; younger pupils learned a verse or two. Many who have since graduated have told me how grateful in retrospect they were, although they didn't always enjoy the discipline at the time! One of our young women told me that in an interview for a job she was asked a particular question and a memory verse came back to her mind which gave her the key! The Word also has power, when stored in the heart, to empower us to avoid sin. "How can a young man keep his way pure? By living according to your Word ... I have hidden your Word in my heart that I may not sin against you."[5]

Shaping the Character

The word of God is intended, as Moses said, to be our very life[6]. It also shapes life through the mentoring of character. The 'one another' verses deal with our responsibility to abandon self-centredness and care for others: 'serve one another'; 'love one another'; 'bear one another's burdens'; 'forgive one another'. (For more see Appendix 6.)

As we sow these principles like seeds week by week in our assemblies or devotional

---

5   Psalm 119:9, 11
6   Deuteronomy 32-47

times, we will see character change. There are countless examples of good and bad characters in the Bible to illustrate these qualities. David and Jonathan for friendship and loyalty; Absalom for pride; Abigail for practical wisdom; Abraham and Noah for obedience; Esther for courage; Joseph for perseverance; Daniel for creative wisdom; Jonah and Gideon for overcoming fear etc. It's worth noting how many of the biblical heroes were teenagers when they were called, including many of Jesus' disciples.

Of course, the highlight is when we make an opportunity for our pupils to respond to the word about Jesus Christ as personal saviour. This must never be pressurising or coercive but sensitive to the Spirit and the pupil. Gradually, the words sown will do their work in challenging and changing the heart. Subsequently, the real character formation is enabled to take place as the pupil learns to cooperate with Jesus and the Holy Spirit.

Hearing Means Doing

Whilst reading and memorising the Word of God is good, it is not enough. Putting it into practice will lead to the shaping of character by learned wisdom: the application of what we know with our mind. Jesus' parable of the wise and foolish builders graphically describes this[7]. Many know Jesus' metaphor that the foolish man built his house upon the sand and the wise man built his house upon the rock. But when we look closely, we realise Jesus makes a particular point about wisdom and foolishness. Both men heard his teaching but only the wise man put it into practice. Many heard Jesus teaching but never became his followers because they never applied his teaching to their lives.

It is interesting that the Hebrew word for disobedience means 'careless hearing'. Pupils hearing the word of God must be helped to put it into practice so they are hearing *and* doing—and this is learning that works.

Our teacher of reception class of 4 to 5 year olds used to say that the first lesson the children had to know was that what she said must be put into practice. Next

---

7   Matthew 7:24-29

they had to learn to accept and care for one another, rather than only thinking of themselves.8 Learning how to resolve quarrels and fights is another key step. The Word of God tells us to forgive one another as God has forgiven us.[9] Our experience was that children as young as 4 and 5 years can learn to say "I'm sorry" and "I forgive you". It was heart-warming to see them frequently resolving conflicts by themselves at break-times on the playground.

Not always are conflicts so easily resolved! There are times, as the Bible recognises, when we become angry with someone else, rightly or wrongly. The Word of God says: "Be angry but do not sin."[10] This recognises that anger can be a valid emotion but that it is important to learn to handle it in the right way. Repressed anger is bad for us and builds up resentment and other emotions which, in the long-term, can even be detrimental to mental and physical health. (More on this in Chapter 11.)

Forming a Worldview

Our long-term aim in teaching a Christian curriculum, whatever structure we use, is to develop the pupils' ability to measure all things against the plumb line of God's word. This helps them to use principles of wisdom from it to interact effectively with the challenges they will face in the world. Any worldview provides answers to the big questions of life such as: What is wrong with the world? What is the solution? What is reality—is there a God? What happens when we die? Whilst there are different Christian theological interpretations particularly about Jesus' return and the end-times, Christian answers to the main questions above would have a widely accepted agreement. A biblical worldview maintains that:

1. God is the creator of all life and the universe
2. The purpose of life is to know God and enjoy and serve him (Westminster Confession)
3. Jesus Christ is God's son who came to earth

---

8   John 13:34
9   Ephesians 4:32
10 Ephesians 4:26

4. Because of Christ's sacrifice on the cross, the main problem of man's sin can be changed and redeemed to live rightly according to God's standards
5. Man is to develop creation as a steward for God
6. Christ as King will return to judge the earth
7. There is life after death: for those who have put their faith in Christ, there is life with God, and for those who reject him there is a lost eternity

Once pupils understand their own religion, and then learn about other religious, ethnic or cultural worldviews, they are equipped to respect others; to relate to them and to build harmony in a world that desperately needs it. This, I believe, is for secondary pupils to study.

Truth Is Muddled and Often Compromised

There is a more sober long-term reason for learning and living by the Word. We are educating our children for life in a world which is complex. One ex-Muslim, now a respected Christian theologian said to me: "The battle for the future generation will be over truth. I am much afraid that if our children do not learn the truth in the Word of God, they will be easily deceived."[11] The Word of God enlightens us, challenges us, enriches us, strengthens us, encourages us and sometimes convicts us, but it also prepares us to build our lives securely on the rock in cultures that are often shifting sand, by giving us enduring values and principles.

The Word in Curriculum

Let us not forget that Jesus Christ is the Word of God.[12] He himself said: "I am the Way, the Truth and the Life."[13] This is an amazing statement showing us the way to eternal life. He is saying: "I am true knowledge." We have already seen how every curriculum subject is relevant to God. How, practically, is it possible to use the Word of God in curriculum subjects? The Bible is obviously not a text book. However, it is a book of wise principles and revelation. Our responsibility

---

11 Speaker's identity protected at his request: conversation in a Theological Forum run by Salt and Light Ministries.
12 John 1:1
13 Jon 14:6

as Christian educators is to be wholly conversant with the Word of God and dependent on the Holy Spirit (as described in the previous chapter) to reveal them to us.

In Genesis Chapter 1 we find some statements for aspects of every subject in an integrated way, through the Creation account. Whilst this may seem simplistic, it is nevertheless true. The first three words "In the beginning" are an historical statement — the beginning of everything on earth. Language is here: God speaks his creation and designates nouns for earth, sky, day, night. God said: "Let there be light". This is a demonstration of physics. Number is here with the order of the days and time is recorded: "morning and afternoon". Physical Geography is evident as God creates the land masses. Biology and botany are represented through the creation of plants. Anthropology is found in verse 28 with the creation of man and woman. Ethics is evident in God's judgement of what he has made, when he evaluates it as 'good'.

Throughout the Bible there are references to different subjects and, importantly, there are wise principles to be applied from God's word to curriculum. Even a concept of fractions is evident in 1 Corinthians 12:27: 'All of you are Christ's body and each one is a part.' What an interesting way to begin exploring fractions by considering ourselves as a whole entity, yet also a fraction of our church, our family or our school class! St. Augustine said: "Wherever truth may be found, it belongs to its master."

Useful Curriculum Structures

There are different ways of using scripture in our curriculum. We are not advocating the bolting on of a verse for the sake of it. Rather we need to ask questions like: What does this unit of learning reveal about God or his world—what wisdom is to be found here? I listened to an engaging talk by Dr. David Smith[14] on how he teaches the German language and how, through a creative approach, he challenges the stereotype that depicts all Germans in the time of World War II as pro-Nazi.

---

14 Dr David Smith (presently lecturing at Toronto University), seminar at National Institute for Christian Education Research, Christ Church Canterbury University, June 2013

A structure can be of assistance to us. One structure employed by some Christian schools is 'The Creation, Fall, Redemption' structure, which has a key question pertaining to each section. The first is: "What was God's original purpose for … water, the environment, humans, agriculture, trade etc.?" A second question is: "How was God's original plan marred by the Fall of man?" This involves an investigation into how man is spoiling or damaging creation. A third question leads into our responsibility in stewarding God's creation by asking: "What can mankind do to redeem this situation and restore something of God's original purpose?" An obvious example would be the purpose of water in a study of the environment and how man's greed pollutes it through industrial waste etc. This would lead, through the third question into studying ways man can steward his environment more carefully.

"A Way to Wisdom" — Through Heart Concepts

Another simple but meaningful structure also uses three parts. It can be helpful to use John 14:6 to designate these as:

1. The truth to be taught in any lesson (a Bible-based concept known as a 'heart concept')
2. The way to teach it (methodology)
3. The life: knowledge and wisdom understood and applied by the pupil

This structure requires us in the first stage to work out our dependence on God in our planning for his direction and inspiration by praying and asking: "What does God want to reveal through this topic, lesson?" etc. The aim is to consider what would be the concept at the heart of the lesson, i.e. the heart concept.

An Example

More examples will be found in Appendix 4, but a first example is the Water Cycle which is a geographical topic (but in some countries is studied in Science). Stage 1 requires us to find Truth to be taught. What does the Water Cycle show us about God? At the heart of the Water Cycle is God's wisdom in his economic provision of water through re-cycling it. So our heart concept may be: 'The Water

Cycle reveals God's wise and economic provision'. This is a scriptural principle: God provides, but wisely. Interestingly, the Water Cycle is described in Ecclesiastes 1:7: 'All streams flow into the sea, yet the sea is never full. To the place the streams come from, there they return again.'

All heart concepts need to be succinct: ideally one sentence. They must be biblically based. They may be a verse of the Bible but most often they need to be re-packaged in language suitable for the age and understanding of the pupils.

The Water Cycle as a geographical or scientific process is taught as it would be in any school. But our question has revealed the wisdom of God behind it: this is a truth to be taught in addition to the Water Cycle process itself.

Stage 2: 'The Way to teach' is the experience of every teacher who must choose the way to teach it asking: "What method shall I use? How will I demonstrate? How shall I plan the learning steps of this lesson?" An important question is: 'Where in the lesson will I choose to reveal the heart concept?'

Stage 3: 'The Life'—wisdom for life. Here another question is explored. "What do I want the pupils to understand and apply?" (Application is a function of wisdom in how to apply our knowledge in life.) Obviously, we want pupils to understand and to be able to explain the Water Cycle. However, we also want them to understand our heart concept which leads us to further wisdom. In this process God is recycling water. As we discuss this and its implications, we can apply our knowledge further: "In what other ways does God use re-cycling in his creation?" Many examples will be found, including the caterpillar-butterfly cycle, plants fruiting and re-seeding and the nitrogen cycle (for secondary pupils).

I and two other colleagues developed 21 Heart Concepts to provide a starting guide for us in understanding some basic aspects of God's wisdom. These include aspects such as Stewardship, Interdependence, Unity and Diversity etc. (See Appendix 3 for the list and for guidance on developing the lesson plan). The "Way to Wisdom" model is used by many schools in different countries. I have been asked many times to produce a text book of heart concepts. However, this would defeat the object of each of us needing to have the joy and privilege of working in partnership with the Holy Spirit: becoming a rightly dependent teacher, as modelled by Jesus. When we get God's revelation for our lesson, topic or theme it gives us enthusiasm and we teach with a fresh vitality. However, I have produced a sample of a variety of heart concepts for different ages and subjects (see Appendix 4).

The heart concept must be biblically sourced but it may not be an actual verse. It becomes a seed of truth to be planted somewhere in the lesson. Teachers must avoid preaching a sermon in every lesson. The heart concept must be revealed and explored but the geography lesson must remain essentially a geography lesson, just as the maths lesson should be essentially about maths.

In order to provide other examples for a secondary lesson we can discuss 'Growth of the British Empire', which is included in some history syllabi. The heart concept here became: 'Man-made empires are always founded on greed and pride, and so always fall, despite the fact that God uses them for his purposes. The Kingdom of God, however, is founded on service and sacrifice, and will never end.' 'In the time of those kings, the God of heaven will set up a kingdom that will never be destroyed, nor will it be left to another people … it will itself endure forever.'[15] As frequently is the case, this heart concept gives breadth to the topic studied, setting it in a wider context.

Such concepts increase our pupils' wisdom and give them a different and more wide-ranging perspective so that they can gradually formulate a biblical worldview to engage with the world.[16]

---

15 Daniel 2:44
16 For more on Curriculum explore 'Foundations for Life' available at The King's School, Witney or HighLight's book 'Aiming for Wisdom' available from office@highlightonline.org

Chapter Eleven
Wisdom in Discipline

Our pupils, our gems, need shaping like all precious stones! Here are two different scenarios which contrast two different ways of dealing with difficult pupils.

Shaping the Diamonds

Jamie stood sullenly beside the headteacher's door; his face black as thunder; his school tie askew; his shirt hanging out. He was in trouble again, and he knew it. He had just been forcibly ejected from Mr Taylor's math's lesson for yet again refusing to cooperate with the math's teacher's instructions. Jamie's stubbornness had escalated from an argument with the whole class as audience, to a 'full-on' rebellion when he had 'lost it'; swearing and shouting at the teacher.

The heels of Mrs Jones, headteacher, tapped out a menacing staccato as she strode purposefully up the corridor towards Jamie.

Scenario 1
Jamie saw with a quick glance from under his eyebrows that she was red in the face and angry. He was in for it now! He kept his head down focusing on the linoleum floor "You again!" she shouted as she drew near, "What have you done this time?"

Jamie could feel her frustration hitting him like a wave. He gritted his teeth and kept quiet, refusing to look up.

"Get in there!" she snapped, flinging the door open so hard it slammed against the filing cabinet.

"Now," she panted, confronting him, "you speak to me this instant—do you hear? What have you done?"

Without looking up he handed her the report slip from Mr. Taylor.

"So," she continued, scanning it quickly "you've been rude to Mr. Taylor and not done your homework?"

"Ugh" he grunted. "But it was too hard, anyway; there was trouble at home."

"Excuses, excuses," she cut in sarcastically, "always excuses. Look at me when I'm talking to you!"

He raised his eyes reluctantly, choosing to gaze over her shoulder defiantly before dropping them again. Boy! Her face was red!

"And you swore at your teacher! I won't have it, do you hear, I won't have it!" Her last phrase ended in a shriek.

"You're no good, Jamie Dunston—you've been trouble since day one, you're lazy and rude. Mr Taylor is a good maths teacher."

Her words stung him into action. He shouted "He hates me, he's always down on me—he pushed me out—I'm reporting him. I've told you, it wasn't my fault. How many more times? There was trouble at home! And I hate you too!"

"That's enough?" she snapped, "you are now on temporary exclusion; the next time it will be permanent. Go to the lobby—I'm ringing your parents to pick you up."

"Good!" he shouted, "exclude me. I can't wait to get out of here!"

He stormed out of the room muttering under his breath "You old cow!"

Scenario 2: This scenario demonstrates a Christian approach.
Jamie glanced up quickly and saw that Mrs Jones was looking very displeased. He was in for it now. He kept his head down focusing on the linoleum floor.

"Jamie—go in," she said calmly, opening her door. "Now sit down," easing herself into her swivel chair.

"What's the trouble? You seem to be outside my door too often." Her voice was friendly, which surprised him, and her tone was patient and concerned. He handed her the report slip.

"It's Mr. Taylor, he hates me." He muttered his eyes down and refusing to meet her gaze by keeping his eyes down.

"Jamie, look at me." She said gently. He looked up unwilling and saw, to his surprise, that she didn't look angry.

"What happened?"

"I'm no good at maths. Mr. Taylor only likes the bright ones."

"It says here you didn't do your homework. Why was that?" she asked, not commenting on his accusation.

"He wouldn't understand" grunted Jamie, "Me mum and her partner Joe had a row and when I stood up for me mum he shouted at me—he's not my dad, so we had a punch-up."

"So the homework never got a look in," she inserted, "That's understandable. But it says here you swore at Mr. Taylor—is that true?"

"Yes," he admitted, "I lost my rag and then he sent me out."

"Jamie, let's unpack this. First of all you say that Mr. Taylor hates you and favours the bright ones."

"Yes—it's true." He said defensively.

"Alright we will have a talk together with Mr. Taylor at lunchtime. Now," she continued, "let's tackle the homework issue. I understand with the trouble at home you couldn't get it done. I'm sorry you had such an upset." She added.

Jamie was surprised she understood! He was calming down now.

"But what should you have done?"

"I should have got a note from me mum explaining it." he admitted.

"That's right," she said, "now let's discuss your response to Mr. Taylor—what do you think about that?"

"I shouldn't have sworn at him and lost me rag," he admitted slowly, "but," excusing himself, "he doesn't like me anyway so I don't like him."

"OK, Jamie, but we are going to talk this out with him. Now go tidy yourself up and go to the library for the last quarter of an hour before lunch when we'll meet with Mr. Taylor."

Jamie grunted a 'thank you' and went off.

They met together. Mr. Taylor, like Mrs Jones, was calm and heard out Jamie's explanation without comment. Afterwards he said, "I'm sorry things are so bad at home Jamie, but you should have explained to me."

"You wouldn't have understood—you only like the bright ones anyway."

"You should have tried me" said Mr. Taylor, "and it's not true Jamie, that I only like the bright ones. I want to help you and others who struggle, but you must ask for help—you never ask. I'm for you Jamie," he stressed leaning forward. Jamie met his earnest gaze and was rocked—it seemed like he meant it.

"Now Jamie," said Mrs Jones, "Do you think an apology is in order? You were very rude to Mr Taylor."

"Yes," he admitted. "I'm sorry Mr. Taylor. But I don't like maths!"

"I forgive you, let's put it behind us. I know you find it hard but we have to work together and if you'll admit it when you need help we could make progress. You may be surprised." He smiled.

Jamie was beginning to feel better—perhaps Mr. Taylor wasn't so bad after all.

"Now Jamie," said Mrs Jones, "the whole class heard and witnessed your rudeness. What do you think you should do?"

"I could apologise to Mr. Taylor in front of 'em, I suppose." He answered soberly.

"Yes, I think that's only right—and what about the homework?" she added.

She wasn't letting him off the hook Jamie thought, but he couldn't help respecting her fairness and her steady, calm approach.

"If Mr. T can explain it, I'll have a go at it tonight," he replied.

"Good," said Mrs Jones and Mr. Taylor together, smiling at this stereo approach.

"By our normal standards I should suspend you Jamie as this is a serious breach of conduct and it's not the first time. But, because of the difficulties you're going through at home, I'm going to give you another chance."

"Thank you!" he gasped in surprise.

"Jamie, if you want help with the situation at home, we can arrange for you to talk it through with a counsellor."

"Thanks," he answered, surprised, "I'll think about it."

"Once you've put things right with the class and tackled the homework we'll put this behind us Jamie," she said, meeting his gaze. "You are more important than the work. We're for you and if you'll co-operate with us we can really go places."

She really means it, he thought.

"Thanks, Mrs Jones, thanks. Thanks Mr. Taylor. I'll give it a go." he said with relief.

"You're dismissed—get some lunch." she said opening the door. He went out feeling so differently to how he had come in. He felt as light as air!

Why the Difference?

What is the reason for the different approaches to these two scenarios? And how is it in the first, a rebellious Jamie is confirmed in that rebellion and all relationships fragmented, whilst in the second the issues are resolved and relationships actually strengthened?

The difference is that the second is based on biblical principles which are redemptive, and offer more possibility of bringing about reconciliation and restitution. The first, however, is non-relational and attempts to deal with anger by meeting it with anger and frustration. Each person is speaking only out of their own strength and emotion: the result—disintegration.

What Is Discipline?

Discipline is not a popular word these days; it carries at worst the connotations of harsh Dickensian punishment, or at least, unpleasant restrictions. The acceptable modern phrase now is 'Behaviour Management' but this does not convey the right meaning. We don't want to simply manage behaviour; we want to nurture, correct and guide our children to maturity in order that they can live positive lives. The root of the word 'discipline' is disciple—to mentor. This involves a relationship of unconditional acceptance, encouragement, guidance and correction—and sometimes there are consequences of wrong actions to be faced.

The key word aligned with discipline in a Christian school context is 'grace'. Grace means undeserved favour or even kindness—when you deserve the opposite!! This doesn't seem to go with discipline but, in fact, it is an essential ingredient. Some years ago, I took my wife to see 'Les Miserables', the musical opera based on Victor Hugo's classic novel. In the first scenes I was impacted by the grace of God. The story begins with Jean, a poor man who is made to work on the chain gang in the 18th century in France. His crime? Stealing bread for his hungry children. In the story he is released after serving his time and again is arrested for stealing food. A priest offers to take charge of him from the police and brings him to his home and feeds him, treating him with great kindness. However, Jean, although deeply touched, falls into temptation, stealing the priest's silver goblets. Arrested again and brought to face the priest, Jean is overwhelmed when the priest says in effect: "Welcome back, son. All I have is yours. Please have my silver candlesticks too." This is grace when we deserve the opposite.

How can this be part of discipline? Surely, we must punish wrong doing? Yes, there are consequences to deliberate wrong doing which involves punishment through deprivation or loss of privileges but in a Christian school context, all must be flavoured with grace. Our pupils are not yet mature and younger children especially need time to learn self-control. Although we had a measure of grace when we began our school, we did not have the fuller revelation that we gained later.

To return again to the story of Adam and Eve and their disobedient act in the Genesis story, we will find we can learn much about discipline from the way that Father God responds to their disastrous choice. Real love must be a free-will choice. To test their love, God had given them freedom to eat of any tree except one in the Garden of Eden where he set them to learn how to steward the planet. They could eat of any other of the abundant and varied fruit trees in this wonderful place. Eve was tempted by Satan, who, in the form of a serpent, suggested to her that God was withholding knowledge from them, which could be gained by eating of the forbidden tree. When Eve repeated the warning God gave to Adam that, if they ate of this tree, they would face the consequence and die, then, as we saw in earlier chapters, Satan deliberately contradicted Eve with the tempting words: "You will not surely die. For God knows when you eat of it your eyes will be opened, and you will be like God knowing good from evil."

When Eve saw the fruit of this tree was attractive and desirable for gaining wisdom, she and Adam took some and ate of it. This choice brought them under Satan's rule and what the Bible calls 'the reign of sin and death'. Immediately, sin entered their hearts and they became self-conscious, desiring to cover up. When God enters the garden, as was his custom, to enjoy fellowship with them they no longer ran to greet him but hid.

God, of course, already knew what had happened and which trees they were hiding behind! He calls them to face him. It is interesting that, as every parent and teacher will know, a younger person who has committed some act of wrongdoing will not look you in the eye! They are 'hiding', just like Adam and Eve.

Pointers from Father God's Approach

God's response and the way he disciplines can give us some valuable guide lines for us. These helped us to develop our own approach to discipline which is depicted in the diagram later in this chapter. We call it 'The Redemptive Cycle of Discipline'. We've shared this with many parents who have put it to good use and have reported back with gratitude and enthusiasm. "This really works!" they have said. It involves the essential ingredient of grace which is evident throughout the Bible in the way God deals with men and women. We will examine these steps in more detail later. First, let us see how God disciplines Adam and Eve.

God Disciplines with Grace

1st Step: Accountability

God requires Adam and Eve to face their act of disobedience. Note, however, he doesn't shout or accuse. God says, in effect: "What is this you have done?" He asks Adam: "Have you eaten of the tree I commanded you not to eat from?"

Adam's audacious reply is breath-taking. He virtually blames God for giving him Eve and takes no responsibility!

2nd Step: Owning responsibility

By contrast, when we face a student with their disobedience the next step is to help them to own it.

God does not react to Adam's reply but, because he, the governor of the earth, blames the woman, God seems to respect this and asks Eve. Eve's answer is more truthful than Adam's although she doesn't properly accept the blame. "The serpent deceived me and I ate." Without answering God judges the serpent who he knows is responsible. Its punishment is clearly a curse involving enmity with mankind which it had spoiled. However, right here in the midst of this awful scene, grace appears. God makes a promise which Adam and Eve and generations to come laid hold of in hope and faith. He promises that one day an offspring of the woman will destroy Satan. This was to be many hundreds of years later but Jesus, conceived by the Holy Spirit, and born of a woman would destroy Satan through his sacrifice on the Cross. This redemptive act was already in God's heart to rescue mankind from the disastrous consequences of Adam and Eve.

God continues to bring his wise judgement to Adam and Eve. The judgement outlines the consequences of their disobedience. This is important, because although it's not spoken at this point, God's forgiveness would mean he would later not abandon man and woman. Not only would he send his Son to express that forgiveness, but he would cause some men and women to search for God and please him. The consequences apply to Adam and Eve's separate spheres and functions. For Adam the earth is now cursed and will not yield easily. In addition, Adam is reminded of the penalty about which God warned him—one day he will die instead of living for ever. Eve will now face more pain in childbirth than was apparently meant to be the case and there will be tension in her relationship with Adam.

Note, however, in all of this, God does not destroy them, nor lose his temper or shout. This, too, is grace. However, there is more to come. With kindness they do not deserve, God covers their sin with his forgiveness by creating more suitable garments for them than flimsy fig leaves! Presumably, the first animal sacrifice yielded these skins. Grace does not end here. The account in Genesis reveals to us that God has more mercy on them. He saves them from having to live forever in their sin and becoming the most despised and hated people on the earth. He banishes them from the garden.

I used to think this was done in anger but my perception has changed. God verbalises the fact that banishing them is a protective measure. If they remained they would eat of the Tree of Life (of which until now they have not partaken). This is the Tree of Everlasting Life. In gracious kindness God removes them from this possibility. Later Eve knows God's help, even though their sin has destroyed intimacy with a holy God. She says: "With the Lord's help I have brought forth a man." No doubt she hoped there would be the promised saviour. It was not yet to be. From this story we learn not to accuse in anger, condemn or lose our temper. We will now follow the redemptive cycle.

The Redemptive Cycle

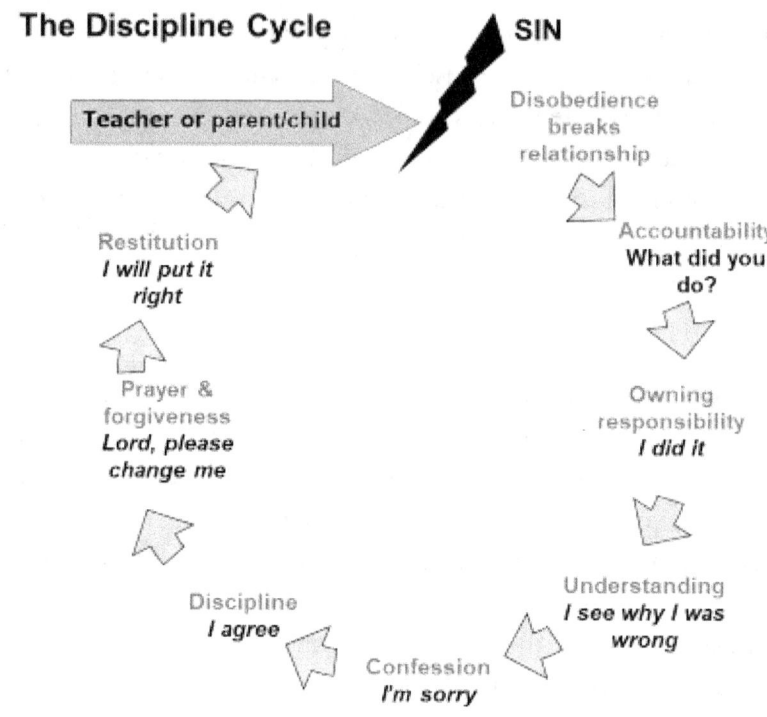

This cycle is mainly to be used for deliberate disobedient acts although it does also apply in smaller issues. In the cycle, the top horizontal arrow represents the relationship between teacher and child, or parent and child, proceeding in harmony. At some point the child disobeys and, where this is deliberate, possibly even after a verbal warning, the disobedience temporarily breaks the relationship. The pupil can no longer meet our eyes—they know they have done wrong and feels guilty, even though they may not be willing to face or recognise it.

Step 1: Accountability
The first step needs to be 'accountability'. As with Adam and Eve, the teacher or parent needs to ask: "Did you do this?" It may have been a reported incident or we may have witnessed it. It is important to keep a level, calm tone of voice

and ask the question. This places responsibility on the child and calls them to account. They will either own up, in which case, we can move to the next step, or, they will say they did not do it. At this point we need to know if the disobedient act has been witnessed by a third party, not just an offended second child. If it was witnessed, we can say so and if necessary produce the witness. At which point the guilty child will normally accept their guilt.

What do we do when there is no witness and the accused denies doing anything wrong? If, after careful questioning and encouragement to tell the truth, they still deny it, we have no choice but to accept their denial. However, we have a secret weapon—the ambush prayer! We now pray that, if they are guilty, they will repeat a similar offence but that there <u>will</u> be witnesses! God answers this prayer! He does so because he wants the guilt exposed for the ultimate good of the culprit! We had a watch stolen in our school and I was fairly sure I knew who had taken it. Questioned with other children, the boy denied it. As a staff we prayed the ambush prayer. In this case he didn't repeat the offence but his guilt weighed so heavily upon him that he owned up after three weeks!

Step 2: Owning responsibility
It is important for the guilty child to own responsibility, which is what Adam refused to do. It is typical to pass the blame on to someone else. I once had a young boy who had thrown a stone at another. He repeatedly claimed his friend had told him to do it, so it wasn't his fault. I had to ask: "Whose hand picked up the stone?" "Mine" he answered. Then, "Whose hand threw the stone?" Again he answered, "Mine". Then the penny dropped as I asked: "So whose fault was it?" "Mine" he admitted, owning his responsibility. We had to deal with his friend too for inciting him to the dangerous action!

Step 3: Understanding
This step can often be missed. We need to check, especially with younger children, that they fully understand why it was wrong and we need to help them face the consequences that could have occurred because of it, as in the case of a careless stone thrown which could have blinded someone. We need the guilty child to say: "I understand why it was wrong".

Step 4: Confession and Repentance

This needs to be a heartfelt "I am sorry I did it"—not a muttered "sorry" through gritted teeth. It may be that the child needs time to calm down and consider their guilt. This especially applies where two children have been angrily fighting each other. It is vital to give a cooling off period for emotions to subside and for reflection.

Step 5: Consequence/Discipline

At this point we need to be listening to the Lord for the amount of grace to be shown. For some children, especially on a first serious offence, this procedure is enough and they have learned their lesson. Hear what is a just consequence. It may be that they lose a privilege or some free time or it may be there is a practical act of repentance that is appropriate.

Step 6: Prayer and Forgiveness

Forgiveness needs to be expressed by the teacher or parent. Forgiveness will also need to be given by the injured party—but they may need counselling and time to be willing to forgive. We cannot force this step. It is important for the offender to ask God's forgiveness, especially if they are a Christian and for us to pray forgiveness to them.

Step 7: Restitution

Where possible there may need to be restitution. The offender may need to apologise to a teacher, an adult or another child, possibly even the whole class. If something was stolen or broken it needs to be returned or replaced.

Step 8: Restoration and Restitution

We have now completed the restoration of relationship. The child needs to know the incident is resolved and can now be forgotten. It may be appropriate to give the child a hug or an older student a brief hand of approval on the shoulder.

In all, this procedure may take only 10-20 minutes depending on how quickly the offender responds. It is important for them to be humbled but not humiliated. The process, where possible, should take place in private (but with a door left open in any separate room—guard against a male teacher being closeted alone with a female pupil and vice versa, especially where dealing with teenagers).

Discipline is, of course, not only dealing with deliberate incidents; it is an atmosphere we set and maintain—an atmosphere of order and grace. Pupils should know what is expected of them and be called up to these standards. I am not in favour of lists of rules but prefer clear expectations which are expressed positively. They do need to know where the boundaries are—this will give them security even if they push or break them! We need to distinguish between major and minor offences. Ideally, this should be consistent as a policy throughout the school.

These need appropriate sanctions. "Make the punishment fit the crime."

Offences

Major	Minor
Persistent or wilful disobedience	Forgetfulness
Rebellion	Unpunctuality (unless persistent)
Bullying	One-off failures
Stealing	
Lying	
A moral violation	

Classroom Tips

The following are tips for maintaining a positive and disciplined working environment.

1. Don't be a nagging teacher. Give one warning: then take action and carry out your warning. (Make sure it was possible for you to enforce it!)
2. Don't label a pupil negatively: e.g. "a pain" or "a nuisance". This becomes a curse.

3. Ask God to give you 'love' (unconditional acceptance) for even the most demanding pupils. They will know if you don't have the right heart for them.
4. Set the atmosphere you want. It helps to lead a class into a classroom rather than allowing then to set a less positive atmosphere before you arrive.
5. Be proactive not reactive; be a responder not a reactor.
6. Stay cool and unshakeable—even if you are not!
7. Answer misbehaviour with a calm tone. An angry tone may incite further rebellion, especially with teenagers.
8. Do not ask general questions e.g. "Has everyone finished?" "Do you all have paper?" This encourages calling out which we want to avoid.
9. Insist on the 'hands-up' rule unless encouraging a debate or free discussion.
10. The 'back-row syndrome'—ensure the back row is for trustworthy pupils. (I have frequently seen the most inappropriate mischievous pupils allowed to sit at the back!)
11. Always insist on pupils looking at you when you are talking. If they are not looking they are not usually listening or learning!
12. Differentiate workload appropriate to ability so all have opportunity to succeed at their level.
13. Clap your hands or find some other means of gaining attention rather than shouting.
14. Set an acceptable noise level which suits you. If necessary, after a warning, insist on a few minutes' silent work until they regain the right to talk amongst themselves.
15. Try to be consistent and fair to all: avoid favourites. (It always backfires.)
16. Give masses of encouragement and constructive feed-back. Pupils do far more right than they do wrong: we just don't notice. Take care to reward your average, quietly consistent pupils.

Discipline is a huge subject. Books have been written about it so in this one chapter we have attempted to cover some major areas. We cannot teach without good order. We have, however, to earn respect by having just and biddable teachers who are also prepared to be humble enough on occasions to say: "I'm sorry. I got that wrong. Please forgive me." Once discipline is in place the whole teaching and learning experience will be hugely enjoyable and rewarding and your community will be more peaceful and secure; but you may have to persevere to reach this state! In the next chapter we examine our role as a Christian community.

Chapter Twelve
The Diamonds in Their Setting

What sort of community should the school be?

Every school is a community. The 'atmosphere', or 'ethos' of that community, is set by the headteacher, the staff and the children. Of these, the headteacher and his/her leadership team are of key importance. I once worked in a school where the Head was a bustling, restless, and frequently combative sort of personality. As a result, the whole school was in tension and the staff was alienated by him.

What should a Christian school's ethos look like?[1]

'Ethos' is a Greek word meaning 'character'. It is used to describe the guiding beliefs or ideals that characterise a community. It has been defined as 'The characteristic spirit or attitudes of a community, people or system.'[2] Ethos sets the 'culture' of the school which is formed by the vision and values of the head and staff. It results in an 'atmosphere' permeating the whole school. The ethos embraced by the headteacher and staff, therefore, sets the climate and outlook of the school—for good or ill.

The ethos or culture encompasses a set of values which the school aims to promote

---

1 Parts of this chapter are extracts from the HighLight booklet: What does a Christian ethos look like in School? Used by permission.
2 Concise Oxford Dictionary

across its curriculum. These values need to be demonstrated and imparted to staff who also own them and impart them to pupils. New staff must be carefully inducted into the importance of the vision, values and ethos of the school. Staff appraisals ensure that teachers are held accountable to the promotion of the school's values in their teaching wherever possible.

The Department for Education lists a positive ethos as a key to success and states: 'A positive school's overall ethos provides all members of the school community with a safe and respected environment, and is paramount in obtaining a successful learning environment.'[3] A positive ethos has been identified in many school improvement studies as being fundamental to raising achievement. Conversely, a negative ethos undermines the success and community of any school. A headteacher who proclaims values of care and consideration for individuals, for instance, but operates in a different spirit produces a cynical staff and pupils. Disunity is the resulting ethos.

The Key Factor

Whilst government directives also affect the boundaries set, sometimes positively and sometimes negatively, I would maintain that the key factor determining the ethos of a school, or any organisation, is the guiding vision, atmosphere and culture that the leader sets and the quality of that leader. In a study of 22 successful schools in the UK, in every case, the most critical factor contributing to their success was the vision of the headteacher.[4]

The ethos and vision will be determined by the beliefs and values of the leadership. Any such vision of the headteacher (and accompanying values) needs to be owned by, and expressed through, his/her leadership team, individual members of the staff team and also owned by pupils. Where this ethos is embraced and based on the right moral principles, success results, not only in academic terms but in terms of pupil character development.

---

3   DfE website: www.education.gov.uk/schools/leadership/schoolethos
4   Excellence in Education: the making of great schools by Cyril Taylor and Conor Ryan: Pub. Fulton

Contrasting Case Studies Based on Fact

1. The headteacher in a certain Primary school was impatient, fiery in nature and always in a hurry. Decisions were made without principle. As a result progress was erratic and depended on his mood or whim. The ethos set by him meant that the whole staff and school were tense and on edge without a clear commitment to a common vision; they also had little respect for him

2. The headteacher in another all-age school was relaxed but firm, modelling and promoting a set of values which encouraged integrity and personal responsibility. This head teacher cultivated warm relationships with staff and pupils; as a result the ethos set was positive, peaceful and harmonious.

Where a headteacher sets an holistic approach as in the 2nd example above; where every individual is valued; where teaching is of a high quality to motivate and enable not only learning but also spiritual, moral, social, emotional and physical learning to take place; the ethos is up-building and generates positive results in many areas. Where, by contrast, a head and staff are *only* academic success-oriented, there will be disillusioned pupils who, because of their limitations, are not valued in any other way. As a result, perceived failure generates a downward spiral and a divided school. Surely preparation for life must be more rounded than this?

The Headteacher

The headteacher needs to be one who has vision, a sense of calling, a servant heart and one who carries the confidence of parents. Every headteacher has a unique personality and gifting. Some will be more administrative than others, some will function more intuitively. However, the following are key principles to aim for:-

- ◊ Be a person who is at peace—even when things are challenging! The school 'ship' needs a steady hand on the steering wheel—especially in times of storm, which will come!

- ◊ Aim to be a responder rather than a reactor. A responder takes time to assess a situation and refuses to rush into action. A reactor may jump to a 'kneejerk' reaction and later regret their haste. Often when a problem arises and you are not sure what to do it is best to sleep on it. Frequently, I have found God gives either a new perspective the next day, or fresh evidence or information becomes available, helping one to see the solution.

◊ Get your vision clear from God. This applies to big vision for your whole school's purpose: Vision and Mission Statements (See Appendix). It also applies to termly focus. In the holidays ask God: "What are the priorities for the next term?" My own priority was to hear from God in what direction to take our devotional theme (e.g.s in Appendix). This would then dictate the content of some of our teaching assemblies; the scripture passages we would learn together and which guest speakers would be appropriate.

◊ Communicate clearly. As noted earlier, the most important ingredient in a successful school is the vision of the leader <u>and</u> his/her ability to communicate it. Communication, or lack of it, is often a major source of frustration. Write down your vision, mission and values—share it at different levels with your governing board, your staff and your parents. Let them shape it and own it. Keep speaking it out and 'putting flesh on the bones' at subsequent meetings. Write it in parent letters. When planning termly vision, get the direction and main ideas from God but then consult.

◊ Be a head who remembers! Keep a notepad with you all the time so that you jot down points the staff and pupils will ask of you on your rounds! Take time to communicate carefully with your deputy or heads of departments and with your administrator. Such regular clear communication ensures smooth running of the school with all on board being secure and clear about the direction they are to go in.

◊ Principles and expectations rather than rules. I discouraged lists of rules in school. As a staff we decided together on key principles for behaviour standards, acceptable character development and code of discipline—again write these down for staff so all can see and know the guidelines for discipline decisions to be made; about which issues are major and which are minor and the appropriate punishments or responses to which all staff need to adhere (even though, due to their personalities, there will be some variations in their classes). I ask teachers to have expectations which they verbalise with children—especially at the start of a new term and at the beginning of a new week—and not too many at once!

- ◊ Open door policy. As head, we need to be accessible—frustrating as it can be when you have so much work to do. For staff and parents to know you can be reached will lead to greater harmony. However, a good administrator will also be sensitive in discerning just how accessible you are on any occasion.

- ◊ Know what is going on in your classrooms. The wise headteacher will avoid being trapped in the office and will visit classes regularly to assess what is happening 'on the ground'. This is taking the 'pulse' of the body!

- ◊ The 'family that prays together stays together'. This adage carries a measure of truth. The school is a spiritual community and prayer by the staff on a regular basis is key to inviting God to sift through problem situations, calling on him to intervene. This builds faith and releases worry and tension from the staff.

- ◊ A Kingdom community. The Kingdom of God is the only community which truly values the weak, vulnerable and less able. This is because a truly Kingdom community will reflect the heart of the King. Colossians 3 gives us a list of qualities to aim for in our class and whole school community. We want to encourage: compassion; kindness; humility; gentleness; patience; forbearance; forgiveness; love.

- ◊ Delegation. Heads should ultimately do what *only they* can do and delegate the rest. Delegation is a key for less stress and a factor in causing staff to grow into their giftings through more responsibility. It requires trust and clear points of accountability. Regular staff appraisals ensure workloads are properly balanced and duties prioritised.

Other Key Principles

What are key principles head and staff should be aiming towards?

It is necessary to remind ourselves again that, in education, as in everything else, Christians are commanded by Jesus Christ to 'seek first the Kingdom of God and his righteousness' (Matthew 6:33). This guides us to educate, lead and run our schools in a way that pleases the King (Jesus) and works out the principles we find in his word. It is unfortunately true that the principles of the Kingdom can be applied vigorously and legalistically but without love. It is possible to visit schools where this is sadly the case and it provokes the worst sort of rebellion in the pupils.

Love: The heart of the community is to be one of love. As we saw in Chapter 7 the word 'love' can have many connotations: we want an atmosphere of unconditional acceptance of each individual—but not necessarily of every type of behaviour! There must be boundaries and yet grace. Grace is shown because we love. In the Colossians 3 list it says that love binds all the other qualities together in perfect unity. Unity is the result of everyone feeling secure in their value and place in the school community. Many of our parents became voluntary part-time helpers or teachers and many discovered a real fulfilment and new giftings.

Worship: At the heart of the community is worship where we express love to the One perfect being in all the universe who is described in the terms: "God is love".[5] In worship we give and receive his love. We learn more about what it means to love. The letter of 1 John defines love for us as God's act of sending his Son to atone as the human sacrifice which could remove our sins. It goes on to say: "No one has ever seen God but if we love one another, God lives in us and his love is made complete in us".[6]

Learning to worship the invisible God takes practice; it's what we were made for. Pupils grow to enjoy it, especially where there is no coercion; where there is some variety rather than just one formula and when they can take part in leading with instruments, drama and dance or other movement. Many older junior pupils and some teenagers are gifted to take responsibility and lead the assemblies. They will make mistakes but they will grow in sensitivity. Practising thanksgiving is a vital part of praise and worship and it is counter-cultural in an often cynical and negative culture.

All the qualities listed in Colossians 3 in Chapter 7 are expressions of love being

---

5   1 John 4:16
6   1 John 4:12

lived out. This results in peace in the community as we accept one another and work to resolve the many differences and offences that will naturally occur.

Other Key Principles

- ◊ Recognising the uniqueness and seeking the wholeness and destiny of the individual
- ◊ Word of God—taught, lived & applied—it defines the values—e.g. honesty, humility, excellence (not perfectionism but doing our best) which includes well qualified teachers
- ◊ Discipleship
- ◊ Curriculum which develops a Christian worldview
- ◊ Wisdom as well as knowledge and understanding
- ◊ Understanding right from wrong and practising forgiveness
- ◊ Trinity—experiencing the character of God, depending on the Holy Spirit and enjoying the presence of God
- ◊ Staff and pupils increasingly reflect the character of God
- ◊ Grace—redemptive discipline
- ◊ Servant heart for the community, the world and a heart for outreach (sharing the Good News)
- ◊ Recognising the uniqueness and seeking the wholeness and destiny of the individual
- ◊ Partnership with parents

Several of the principles above have already been discussed in earlier chapters. Attention will now be paid to those principles not yet specifically covered.

Trinity: Experiencing the Character of God, Depending on the Holy Spirit and Enjoying the Presence of God

God chose to be revealed as Father, Son and Holy Spirit. There is a wealth to be explored in scripture of the mystery of God's oneness and three-in-oneness. Each lends themselves to a term's theme or study. God's Fatherhood is of key importance to all, but especially for those who have been bereaved or experienced traumatic family break-up. The revelation of Jesus leads to an understanding of the nature of Father as revealed through his Son and leads to the possibility of receiving him as Saviour and Lord. The Holy Spirit represents the mystery and miraculous power of God, as well as being a counsellor and helper alongside us who leads us into truth.

Partnership with Parents

School can only do so much and should not be expected to do everything. The parents will always be the most important people in our pupils' lives. We need to work to create the very best partnership with our parents through very good communication; listening to their understanding of their child; involving them in the education process; honouring and respecting them and working together on our goals for their children's future character, academic and vocational development.

The Staff

Consistency by the staff and their modelling of love, worship and the above values and principles of the school are vital. Our pupils 'read' our actions and responses; they are quick to notice, and be affected by, discrepancies. Therefore, in interviewing potential new staff, it is important to look for those who sense the call of God themselves and can subscribe to our expressed vision and values. They need to be those who are themselves personally committed to develop their own revelation of, and relationship with, God and who are willing to be teachable. Not only do they need to feel called, there must be a corresponding witness in the headteacher and the interviewing panel also. The important issue is to find the will of God for the candidate, as well as for our school. It is far better for the wrong candidate to be released to find their proper destiny, than for us to appoint out of pressure or sympathy.

The staff will all reflect different aspects of the nature of God: some will be administrative and focussed on the curriculum only; others will be creative, innovative and take risks. The whole range of gifts is needed to give our pupils a rich experience of the variety of human nature reflecting God's image.

The Community Serving the Wider Community

It is common experience that the school affects the immediate wider community for good or ill by its very existence. This can be positive or negative depending on the behaviour and awareness of the students! In the beginning our school got negative press because some neighbours had not wanted a school so close to them. This led to challenges which we had to live through. However, in a few years, the town community began to speak favourably about our students. A frequent comment was: "We can tell your pupils from others by the way they walk down the street, even when they are out of uniform". It turned out that they had better manners and more respect for other pedestrians.

Another factor that swung opinion was our frequent involvement in serving the community—something that still continues today. Servanthood is an important character quality to be practised in the school and in the immediate community outside the school; it turns students away from their preoccupation with themselves and the inherent selfishness in us all and teaches them humility, care for others and faithfulness. We looked for opportunities for our pupils to serve in a school for handicapped children; to do gardening or errands for elderly people and to be regular visitors to a nearby residential home for the elderly. Our junior pupils worked on a local history project which was hugely enhanced by interviewing these residents about their past memories, which the children recorded. They then came and read their work out to the elderly people. A rather special consequence was that, in several cases, relationships with special affection developed between the elderly person and 'their' pupil, so much so, that, the pupils continued their visits beyond the project. We began to be invited to partake in the Lord Mayor's Carol Service and many other such occasions. I believe we were being a positive light in the community.

Pupils Released to the Wider Community

Our pupils completed their GCSEs at 16 and then went on to local comprehensive 6th forms or further education. Very soon, reports came back from staff in these places with comments like: "Your pupils get their work in on time" (that was a surprise—we didn't always seem to experience that benefit!). Another frequent comment was: "Your pupils have something special about them"; and another was: "Your pupils know what they believe and aren't afraid to speak out". More proof of the positive influence was evident when we heard that several of our students were appointed as counsellors to other pupils because of their behaviour and care.

Surely this is what 'education' should be about: learning how to live your life to serve and bless others you meet and other generations? A school can be a 'light' giving encouragement and hope to local citizens in a time when there is so much criminal and negative behaviour in our wider society.

Not all of our pupils were success stories. Some lost their way for a while but we have seen many of them return to faith. The Holy Spirit is faithful to call them back to the faith sown into their lives by parents and teachers. In all of them we believe we have sown principles of truth, a sense of being loved and accepted and an experience that they will value when they look back. This is certainly the case for many we have since met who are now adults. Some said to us of their 6th forms: "At your school we were known and loved—here we are only a number." One girl reported back to me: "Mr Freeman, I'm so glad I was well prepared here because in the new school I have been offered everything from sex to drugs. I'm so grateful our school taught us about these issues so we were prepared."

Controlled Exposure

Our aim in the top three years of our school up to the GCSE exams at 16 years was one of what we called 'controlled exposure' of our pupils to the issues of our culture: ethical issues like abortion, drugs awareness, and other faiths—we did the best we could to prepare them to understand the issues, and what the biblical viewpoints were so that they could then make up their own minds. One of our pupils, who made some wrong choices, told me of her subsequent depression. However, she said that she would frequently call on God, take her Bible out and God never failed to speak through verses she read, until eventually she was ready to ask his forgiveness and return to her faith. Whilst we always fall short and may always feel we could have done more and done it in a better way, God will use our efforts.

Was it worth it? Was there enough fruit? See Chapter 14!

Chapter Thirteen
Life in the River

The Christian school always faces the danger of becoming too set in its ways; religious legalism is one extreme and 'sloppy grace', where things become too loose and unrestrained is the other. How does a school stay fresh and relevant? I believe a huge part of the answer lies in 'staying in the river'.

What do we mean by 'the river'? The river is the life-flow, which comes from God. In Ezekiel 47 we read of this river of life which has its source in the Temple of Ezekiel's vision. The water flowed out of the Temple into the nation. As it flowed, Ezekiel discovered that it became deeper and wider — 'a river that no-one could cross'.[1] Ezekiel is told by the angel that this river makes even the Dead Sea fresh: 'where the river flows everything will live'.[2]

This image of the river of life, also found in Revelation, is a picture of the Holy Spirit who is the Spirit of love, life and wisdom who guides us into all truth.[3] It is good to remember that if, as we have emphasised, we are seeking first the kingdom of God in everything that we do, the Bible tells us that the kingdom of God is 'in the Spirit'.[4]

A headteacher friend of mine, more experienced than I, encouraged me to keep

---
1 Ezekiel 47:5
2 Ezekiel 47:9
3 John 16:3
4 Romans 14:17

praying for the Holy Spirit to flow in our school, especially in our times of worship, but not only there. I was so grateful for this advice. As a staff, and personally, we kept on trusting the Lord Jesus to come by his Spirit.

He came in many varied ways. Often in worship a supernatural peace would rest on the whole assembly—even boisterous young five and six year olds would be at rest. At other times he came in times of exuberant praise and there would be laughter and joy. One of our teachers was especially open to this and laughed a lot with the joy of the Lord, to the pupils' delight! At other times the children learned to exercise faith in the gifts of the Spirit from 1 Corinthians 12. The first time this happened was a surprise to us all. It was a few weeks after we had begun the school and children began to bring words of faith. We had a visiting educator who was totally astonished as he saw children aged 9-13 bringing words of knowledge for healing and praying for one another—especially as he didn't believe the gifts were for this present age!

Let the Children Come Unto Me

Our youngest infants learned in their other assembly times to praise God. Why? Because God likes it! Then, after praise, they would sit and wait quietly and practise listening to God. We were awed by the way God began to give them prophetic pictures and words. It began very simply. After waiting quietly, with their eyes closed, we would ask if anyone had seen anything or had any thoughts to share. Pictures began to be shared very simply. Often they involved a good versus bad object—for instance, a decaying orange and a good one, or a flower in a vase of water and a dying one in an empty container. We would ask the children what they felt God might be showing them; very often they knew and would link these sorts of pictures to how God wanted us to receive his love, or his Spirit. Sometimes we interpreted. We found they had no barriers of unbelief like us! Of course, sometimes they copied another or made up something but, with encouragement, they grew in hearing God.

The most significant word came from a girl who saw a solid bar of pure gold and a flashing diamond. She said in explanation: "The diamond was flashing and saying 'Look at me. Look at me' but it was Satan's trick. The Holy Spirit said: 'Look at the bar of gold which said nothing. The bar of gold is Jesus. He is pure gold.'" We were astounded. Another girl, Sarah (name changed) brought us the following vision. She saw an ugly grey rock sticking out of the sea. "That's my life", Sarah said, without any prompting. Then she saw the rock sink under the sea. "The sea is God's love", she said, "and it's covering my life." The next scene was the rock reappearing on a gloriously beautiful island covered in flowers. "That's how Jesus has made my life beautiful", she said. With the help of a teaching assistant, Sarah painted the three scenes and I have shown them all over the world. Without fail, they impact audiences. Sarah had asked Jesus into her life a couple of weeks earlier and he brought a rather restless, frenetic girl into peace.

Flexibility and Sensitivity

As we seek the King's will as a priority for each day, it is important to ask him to help us remain in his will—which is to remain in the direction the Holy Spirit brings. We will never do this perfectly but this needs to be our prayer and our aim. It is all too easy to move away from an active dependence on God and rely on our own established routines.

Whilst routines are useful, we need to guard against the natural (but fallen!) tendency of our flesh to rely on ourselves, our rationality and our plans. I usually saw it as my role to lead the majority of the assemblies. But sometimes God wanted a change! He knows better than us what our children need. On several occasions I learned that when I could 'get nothing' for an assembly, God wanted to speak through someone else. Alternatively, he might want to direct us through a word of testimony, prophecy or of specific knowledge to focus on an aspect or direction we hadn't considered.

God's promise is that, if our hearts are yielded to him and looking for him in each day and situation, he will show us what to do: "I am the Lord your God, who teaches you what is best for you, who directs you in the way you should go.

If only you had paid attention to my commands, your peace would have been like a river, your righteousness like the waves of the sea."[5]

God Is a God of Surprises

In our larger assemblies there were a few occasions when the river caught us by surprise and flowed more powerfully. At these times our assemblies became longer. Pupils would lie down and enjoy God's presence, sometimes quietly praying for one another. After one such occasion, I asked if God had shown any individuals any particular thing to share with us. Three pupils put their hands up: one said: "God has shown me I'm going to work in India"; a second said: "God has shown me I am going to work with children in Egypt". The third one, a boy, said firmly: "God has shown me he's going to use me to share Jesus in my village".

The Holy Spirit might come powerfully but God is not a God of confusion but of order and peace.[6] We did not allow hysteria or wild behaviour but believed that, whilst there should be freedom, because "the Lord is the Spirit and where the Spirit is there is freedom",[7] there must also be a measure of self-control.

The Word of God

If we only concentrate on the Holy Spirit we are lacking in wisdom. The Lord is the Spirit but he is also the Word of God. In our assemblies and worship we would ensure there was teaching from God's word. In this, I or whoever was to share, was still seeking to allow the Holy Spirit to guide us in what we prepared so we would prayerfully remain 'in the flow' of what the Lord wanted to highlight that day. Before the term began I also planned themes for a term's assemblies. These guided us as a staff each term. Themes included: The Kingdom of God; Faith; The Nature of God; The Story of Abraham and Sarah; or Moses, David, Paul (or other positive Bible characters). Linked with these stories (which we would dramatise with the children in an impromptu way) were relevant memory verses to learn for that week. The Word and the Spirit will give us a balanced

---

5   Isaiah 48:17-18
6   1 Corinthians 14:33
7   2 Corinthians 3:17

walk of faith. As we stay open and dependent for God to lead us we can avoid extremism.

How Do We Stay In the River?

How do we ensure that we keep being filled with the Holy Spirit? It is not complicated or difficult; it is simple: we ask. Father gives to those who ask. "Ask and it will be given you… for everyone who asks receives."[8] As head and staff we need to stand regularly in the presence of God to give our personal praise and adoration and to receive by faith the Father's life-flow: his strength, energy, creativity, wisdom, love and grace. Due to our complicated travel arrangements, we could only manage a short time of about 10 minutes each morning before school started to be in God's presence as a team but it was wonderfully worth it! It focused us and reminded us of who we were serving.

Jesus taught that one drink can release a river! 'Jesus stood and said in a loud voice, "If anyone is thirsty, let him come to me and drink. Whoever believes in me, as the Scripture has said, streams of living water will flow from within him." By this he meant the Spirit, whom those who believe in him were later to receive.'[9] As the teacher drinks, so from him or her flows a river of the Spirit of life for their students. We then teach out of our spirit as well as out of our mind. This does not deny the logical, rational use of our mind (which Jesus also demonstrated on many occasions) but rather enhances those processes with additional revelation, creativity and energy and grace.

The River Flows to the Sea

In the physical world rivers flow to the sea, and so it is in Ezekiel's vision. As our pupils have grown and become mature men and women, many of them married (and one or two called to celibacy), it has been thrilling to find that God has led them all over the world. Many are working in the UK in teaching or caring professions: doctors, nurses, law, business, finance, marketing etc. One became an astronaut! Many are now working in foreign countries. Several are in church

---

8   Luke 11:9-10
9   Luke 7: 37-38

or mission leadership: one in Belgium, one in Spain, one in Florida, another in Canada. One Nigerian girl who studied with us for several years became a lawyer in Lagos. We received her photo complete with judicial wig! Others are in places as diverse as Poland, Florida and Columbia. I'm not sure if the girl who saw herself working in Egypt has got there yet. Another of our boys has steadily prepared himself to go to China and has learned Mandarin!

Early on in the school's life, I purchased a huge wall map whilst in America. It was displayed in the school hall. I felt God prompting me that he wanted us to give our pupils a heart for nations, including our own. As we invited leaders and contacts from other nations to visit our assemblies when they were in England, so the children's horizons and boundaries were widened and stirrings of faith took place in many. In addition, we visited other countries with our senior students. Each summer, those who chose to, saved up, and raised money to go to countries where we as a church or school had links. They have visited Uganda, Zambia, Kenya, China and India. Without fail, these visits have affected their worldview, their values and their view of our comparatively comfortable culture. They come back transformed, having learned to serve, to exercise faith and overcome their fears and prejudices. They are astounded at how children in developing countries can still experience joy from God with very little resources. Many of our students have determined to go and make a difference—and some have done so. Others know their call is to make a difference in the United Kingdom. Everything that is healthy is part of something larger and every stream that remains fresh has an outlet, whereas water that is static becomes stagnant. This outward focus is another healthy, and extremely valuable, dimension of a Christian education.

All of this sounds good but, you may be asking, where is long-term evidence of fruitfulness? When we began our school you will remember that I answered those who were doubtful with the words: "Come back in ten years and we hope we will have some fruit to show you." So did we? In the last chapter we ask: What is the fruit?

Chapter Fourteen

Fruit

In the early days of our school, back in the mid-eighties, I was asked many times questions such as: How do you know this is going to work? How do you know you are not jeopardising the future prospects of these children? What if they don't get good enough qualifications for university or career? The simple answer was that we did not <u>know</u> it would be successful; this was a venture of faith and, because we were human, it carried the risk of failure. I would answer these questions using a metaphor Jesus taught. In the context of warning his disciples about false prophets he said: "Do people pick grapes from thorn bushes, or figs from thistles? Likewise every good tree cannot bear bad fruit, and a bad tree cannot bear good fruit ... Thus, by their fruit you will recognise them."[1] I would answer truthfully (and I hope, humbly): "We don't know. But come back in ten years and we hope we will have some fruit to show you, for Jesus said, 'By the fruit you will recognise the tree.'"

So, after over 30 years, do we have fruit as evidence? It is a fact that even after two years we were so encouraged by the growth—morally, spiritually, socially, emotionally and academically—that we believed we were on the right track. As I have indicated, we were learning a new way to educate and made many mistakes. However, we saw enough positive results to persevere, although the journey was costly in finance and man and woman-power. So many of our pupils, who had

---

1   Matthew 7:16-20

transferred to us from other schools, expressed the fact that it was a relief to them that now everything was, as they put it, ' going in the same direction'. They had clearly felt a huge pressure in living in two, often conflicting, spiritual atmospheres (home and school). Several had felt guilty that, because of peer pressure and the desire to be accepted, they had 'kept their heads down' about issues of their personal faith. One boy who had a lot of fear in his life grew in faith and became bold enough to speak out in assembly. All seemed to grow in confidence in the atmosphere of unconditional acceptance.

Have all our children maintained a faith in Jesus Christ? Many have but we have also had several 'prodigals' who have gone their own way. To balance this, we have, over time, seen many return to faith. Our vision for our pupils to serve God's purposes for their lives has been rewarded in many instances but not in all. God has given free-will to us all and some have not yet followed what we might be considered is the best plan for their lives. However, recently I discovered one of our ex-pupils is serving God in Bogota, Columbia; another in Brazil; another in Florida and another preparing to be a medical doctor in Africa. One is pastoring in Belgium; one in Spain; yet another is leading a newly-planted church in Canada and another is presently heading up a prestigious school in the same country. It is absolutely as important that many are serving in the UK, as businessmen, lawyers, teachers, nurses and a whole variety of other professions; not a few are in church or mission leadership.

What About the Academic Fruit?

Have all our children achieved well academically? Our academic results have always, by God's grace, been high, with an average of over 80% gaining grade A to C. In some years this has been even higher. We have seen over the years that God has fulfilled his promise: 'Those who honour me, I will honour.'[2] Of course, academic results depend on many factors other than the school: amongst them the student's ability and motivation and also the support and encouragement that students receive from parents are of key importance. Over the years we have experienced that students of lesser ability who have tried to do their best have

---

2   1 Samuel 2:30

nearly always gained a grade higher than their teachers anticipated. This seems to us to be the goodness of God and his encouragement to them. For us, as a school, it must be obvious from the previous chapters of this book that, whilst we are committed to a full academic programme, we are also committed to the shaping of character and godly values.

Character and competence could be summarised as our two main objectives in mentoring our pupils. As one preacher once said: "Gifting without character is like a gem in a loose setting; it is easily lost". No matter how gifted the pupil, unless there is integrity of character that gifting and that life can be easily squandered or lost. The pupil as a person is more important than his or her performance! We have compiled a list of character qualities that we desired to sow into our pupils. These can be found in Appendix 6. They are all based on the word of God. By promoting these as part of our values in assemblies, class devotions and in personal tutor times, we will be steadily encouraging, challenging and shaping good character.

Objective "Fruit"

The above is only the fruit from one school. Is there a more objective way of assessing the evidence? I am very grateful for the successful PhD thesis of my colleague, Dr Sylvia Baker. For this research, senior pupils of some 25 of the 'new, independent Christian schools', which opened in the United kingdom from 1970 onwards, responded to a survey questionnaire. This has now been published as "Swimming against the Tide".[3] 695 pupils from Year 9 and Year 11 in these schools responded in 2006 to a wide range of questions assessing their beliefs and values. Areas covered included Religious beliefs, Science and Creation, Personal concerns, Education and School life, Views and Moral values. The latter included views on right and wrong, sexual morality, anti-social behaviour, media influence, substance use, work, politics, global fears and environmental issues. Wide ranging indeed!

---

3   Dr S Baker: Swimming Against the Tide: The New Independent Christian Schools and their teenage pupils: 2013 Peter Lang

What sort of conclusions did this reveal? In final summary Dr Baker writes: 'The initial empirical evidence, provided by the study, suggests that the schools are fulfilling their educational aims while at the same time producing well-adjusted young people with the potential to become good citizens.'[4] The results, Dr Baker emphasises, are an encouragement for the parents and teachers in these schools because the survey showed that the majority (87%) of the young people professed faith in Jesus Christ (75% of their parents were Christians). Moral standards aspired to by the majority of young people are positively Christian. Teachers can be encouraged that in the majority of cases, the young people were happy in school (although a minority were not) and the majority felt that their teachers were doing a good job.

The overall picture is not entirely rosy. A significant 11% of the 695 pupils in these Christian schools claim to have no personal faith and their views are often at variance with the majority. Yet, surprisingly 50% of these still hold a high view of Christianity in that they are not prepared to deny the central doctrines. It also becomes clear that there are other areas for concern: in particular, a worrying view that many of the young people do not regard drunkenness as wrong.

There are some surprising results from the survey. One is that the normally accepted trend for the faith of teenagers to decrease as they grow towards 16 is not affirmed by this survey: to the contrary, the majority of 16 year olds are maintaining their faith. In addition, the normal pattern of the number of young people declining in churches[5] is contradicted by these young people: around 77% regularly attend church and 67% attend every week.

This survey obviously only records teenage values at that given time. More evidence is needed to discover the beliefs and values of present pupils but also of those pupils surveyed now that they are adults. Will the majority still hold the Christian faith and a Christian standard of morality? More research is needed to assess what might be called 'long-term fruit'. From Dr Baker's research there are

---

4   Dr S Baker: Swimming Against the Tide: The New Independent Christian Schools and their teenage pupils: 2013 Peter Lang p.229
5   English Church Census 2005

many fascinating results and there are also implications for parents, teachers and even the government, but you will need to read the book!

The Greatest of All Is Love

I now have the privilege of travelling to many countries in order to share and promote 'the diamonds' of God: the principles shared in this book. Wherever they are applied with faith there is fruit: not because of my ability, but because the principles are inherently good! In the Democratic Republic of Congo I taught the staff of three schools over three days—one of them very poor indeed. It had mud-baked walls making the classroom seem like a dark cave and classes of 80 with one teacher and a blackboard. In the year subsequent to the training, these three schools all came top in their city exams (which they never had before). Is this coincidence? Maybe, but I believe it is because, when the principles are applied with faith and diligence, God honours them.

The 'diamond' that seems to make the biggest difference of all is the principle of unconditional love from teacher to pupil.[6] Pupils have responded to the teachers' encouragement and care and have given their best. Love, God's love, changes lives for the better. Surely, we as school leaders, teachers and parents can ask for nothing better than this: lives transformed and directed by the love of God into their personal destinies.

---

6   See Appendix 6: The Key of Unconditional Acceptance

Appendix 1
Wisdom Quiz
Wisdom in Real Life from the Bible

Answer sheets

Ask yourself: What sort of wisdom is demonstrated here? What can we learn from this?

Task 1 — The Wisdom of Abraham and Nephew Lot
Read Gen 13:5-18

- ◊ On what basis did Lot choose his land? By outward appearances.
- ◊ Was this wisdom? Of a sort, but not the whole picture. It left God out.
- ◊ Did Abraham show any wisdom? If so, when and how? By trusting God. By dealing with the root of the quarrel.
- ◊ Look up the consequences of Lot's choice. Gen 19:12-13, 29. He ended up living in the midst of godless people and he and his family would have been destroyed along with them if it had not been for God's intervention.
- ◊ What can you learn from this? Don't choose by outward appearance; ask God his perspective first.

Task 2 — The Choice of David as King
Read 1 Sam 16:1-13

- ◊ How was Samuel tempted to choose? By outward appearance.
- ◊ Why would this not have been wise? He would have judged by outward appearance — not the true heart.
- ◊ What was it important for Samuel to be able to do in this process? Listen to God.
- ◊ What can you learn from this? Learn to ask God despite what may seem obvious by outward appearances.

Task 3—The Wisdom of Naaman
Read 2 Kings 5:1-14

- ◊ Who did Naaman listen to in the beginning? Servant girl.
- ◊ What caused Naaman to object to bathing in the Jordan? Pride, outward appearance, dirty river.
- ◊ What sort of wisdom was this? Worldly wisdom—intellect
- ◊ What was he concentrating on? Outward appearance of the river.
- ◊ Who shows the most wisdom in this story? Servants.
- ◊ What is the key to Naaman getting healed? Obedience to the word of God.
- ◊ What can you learn from this? It is important to obey God despite our preferences.

Task 4—The Wisdom of the Prodigal
Read Luke 15:11-31

- ◊ What was wrong with the Prodigal son's choice at the beginning? He hadn't thought through the consequences.
- ◊ Look at v. 17-19. What indicates that he became wise? He came to his senses.
- ◊ What was the key to the Prodigal being blessed? Repentance, humility, submission.
- ◊ Read v. 29-30. Do you sympathise with the older brother? Is he speaking wisdom? No—he's only seeking his own point of view.
- ◊ Do you think the father showed wisdom in the beginning and at the end of the story? Yes—in releasing the son to his own will as an adult and then receiving him unconditionally in love and grace.
- ◊ What can you learn from it? Learn to be gracious and forgiving. People often won't be told but have to make their own mistakes—however it is wiser to listen to experienced people's advice.

Task 5 — The Wisdom of Jesus (Lazarus)
Read John 11:1-7, 11-19, 32-44

- ◊ Why did Jesus not hurry straight to his sick friend? God spoke to Him.
- ◊ Why would it not have been wisdom to go to Lazarus straight away? It would have brought less glory to God.
- ◊ What was the key to getting God's wisdom in this story? Hearing God — knowing God's will.
- ◊ If Jesus had healed Lazarus straight away, this would have been a miracle so why wait longer? Reviving him from the dead gave greater glory to God.
- ◊ Do you think Jesus struggled with having to wait? Probably — this was going against culture.
- ◊ What can you learn from this? Wisdom is hearing and obeying God — it might not be what seems the most sensible thing.

Task 6 — The Wisdom of Mary
Read John 12:1-8

- ◊ What were Judas' reasons for objecting to the perfume being poured on Jesus? A waste of money — could sell the perfume and give the money to the poor.
- ◊ Why was his thinking wrong? He was only thinking of the money.
- ◊ How was Mary's action wise? She "knew" in her spirit it was important to do this.
- ◊ What do you think you might have thought if you were there?
- ◊ What does this teach you about judging people's actions? Don't be quick to criticise; the person may be hearing God.

Task 7 — The Wisdom of Jesus in Revival (In Capernaum)
Read Mark 1:32-39

- ◊ What was Simon's reasoning in wanting to stay? Yesterday had been so successful; Jesus should stay and do more.
- ◊ Why do you think Jesus was praying? To find direction from God for the day.
- ◊ What is most important to Jesus? What God is saying.
- ◊ What sort of wisdom was Simon using? What people think.
- ◊ What can you learn from this that it might be wise to ignore? Don't let people pressurise you into decisions.
- ◊ What is a key for success in Revival from this story? Keep hearing and obeying God/Jesus.

Task 8 — The Wisdom of Jesus Versus the Wisdom of Satan
Read Luke 4:1-13

- ◊ On what basis was Satan trying to make Jesus decide in temptation No. 1? The basis of using his power to satisfy his own appetites.
- ◊ What does Jesus' reply mean? God's word is more important than food.
- ◊ What does Satan want in temptation No. 2? Worship—Jesus to submit to him.
- ◊ Do you think that Jesus didn't want the kingdoms of the world? He did want them, but He would have got them the wrong way.
- ◊ In the 3rd temptation, Satan uses scripture. Why is it wrong here? He wants Jesus to use God's power for himself.
- ◊ Why was it vitally important that Jesus did none of the things Satan asked? Because He would have been obeying Satan and disobeying God like the first Adam.

- ◊ What can we learn from Jesus' answers? They are all scripture. Don't discuss with Satan (e.g. Eve)—just know the truth.

Task 9—The Wisdom of Mary and Martha
Read Luke 10:38-42

- ◊ Is Martha wrong to want to prepare a meal for Jesus? No—but she is doing it at the wrong time.
- ◊ Why was Mary not regarded as lazy by Jesus? She was putting higher value on listening and learning from Jesus.
- ◊ What is the "one thing" that is needed? To listen.
- ◊ What can you learn from this? It is not always pleasing to God to be very busy—even when we think it is for him—he wants our friendship and attention too.

Appendix 2
Values

- All values are based on the main value of Love as defined in Chapter 7
- Respect for others: equal respect for men and women and different ethnic origins or sexuality
- Inclusivity: welcoming all
- Care and consideration for others (non-reactive)
- Tolerance means respect for those of other faiths or non-faith without compromising one's own belief
- The intrinsic value of every individual—irrespective of ability or performance
- The uniqueness of every individual
- Justice—upholding the law
- Compassion/mercy for the weak, disadvantaged and the deprived
- Kindness
- Humility
- Judging one's self rather than judging others critically
- Honesty/truthfulness
- Integrity—internal integrity
- The healthy sign of relating wider—external integration
- Redemptive approach to failure especially behavioural but also academic.
- Grace (in relationships)—forgiveness.
- The right vision, ethos, and values lived out by headteacher and staff will create a vibrant and healthy learning environment. We will make mistakes, but by the grace of God and his help, a positive dynamic will be released where very pupil can succeed in different ways and be prepared, as citizens of integrity, to fulfil their destiny in God. The future belongs to those who prepare for it.

Appendix 3
Keys for Wisdom in Curriculum

21 Themes for Attaining Wisdom in Curricular Education

All curriculum is interpreted and conveyed with values. No curriculum is value-free. The following are suggested as principles which are appropriate and lead to increased wisdom.

1. Uniqueness and creativity—PSHEE, RE Art Drama Biology
2. Our wonderful world—Geography, Science, Art
3. Conservation and Responsibility—Ecology, Health, and Medicine
4. Tracing trends in history—Anthropology, History
5. Unity and Diversity—All subjects
6. Order and Structure—Maths, English, MFL, Science, Music
7. Wisdom—All subjects
8. Interdependence—All subjects inc. PE
9. Love and Caring—Community and Health Care, PSHEE
10. Sharing resources—Geography
11. Family—Sociology
12. Integrity—Moral values, PSHEE, Citizenship
13. Justice and Ethics—Law, Moral issues, Science, Citizenship
14. Communication—English Lang. MFL, Media studies
15. Awe and Wonder—Art, Music, Astronomy, Geography, Science
16. Culture, People and Places—Anthropology, History, Geography, Art, Music, Drama
17. Growth and productivity—Biology, Economics, Agriculture, Business
18. Government and Citizenship—Politics, Citizenship, History

19. War, Peace and Reconciliation—History, World Politics, Current issues, PSHEE
20. The Future—RE, Ecology, Science, Geography, Future trends
21. Beliefs—RE, Theology, World religions, Philosophy

KEY: MFL—Modern Foreign Languages

PSHEE—Personal, Social, Health and Economic Education

Wisdom Themes Expanded and Followed by a Contrasting Secular View

Uniqueness and creativity—PSHEE, RE, art, drama, biology
Every individual is uniquely created in God's image; is therefore valuable and able to be creative in different ways.

Gen 1:27-8; Ps 139:13-14

Man evolved by chance.

Our wonderful world—Geography, science, art
The world, earth and universe, was created by God and is full of wonders (both intricate and grand) for us to explore, understand interpret and enjoy.

Gen 1:1; John 1:1-3; Col 1:16-17

Nature and the universe evolved by chance.

Conservation and responsibility—Ecology, health, and medicine
We have a responsibility to care for our planet and to care for each other and especially those in need.

Gen 1:26; Luke 19:11-27; Proverbs 14:31; Phil 2:1-5

We use the world's resources primarily to maintain ourselves. We may choose to benefit others with our surplus. Conservation is important for self-preservation.

Tracing trends in history—Anthropology, history
By studying history we can learn from God's plan and the errors of the past; we can also discover and evaluate trends caused by people or principles so that we can learn from their experience.

Prov 21:30; Isaiah 9:7; Rom 8:28; Acts 17:24-8; Psalm 33: 6-11; Job 42:2; 1 Cor 10

History is only a catalogue of random events.

Unity and diversity—All subjects
Unity and diversity can be found in the Trinity and the same principles are to be discovered in all subjects in different ways. The world is full of diverse peoples. This diversity can enrich others; it can also be a cause of conflict. The principle of unity is desirable in order to help and strengthen one another: when people cooperate there is synergy and benefit. Distinctive and diverse qualities need to be respected.

John 17:20-23; John 14:23-27, 16: 7-15; 1 Cor 12; Romans 12:3-8; Deut 32:30

There is no overall unity or pattern to the universe; it is random; diversity is purely accidental.

Order and structure—Maths, English, MFL, science, music
There is order and structure to be discovered in every aspect of learning; most especially in Languages, Maths, Science, Music and Art.

Gen 1; Isaiah 9:7a; 1 Cor 14:33

There is no overall order or underlying structure in nature; it is continually evolving.

Wisdom—All subjects
True wisdom, as opposed to worldly wisdom, is a gift of God and requires humility, teachability, consequential thinking and the application of knowledge and understanding according to God's code of values; this leads to an appropriate decision or response.

Prov 4:7-8; 9:10; James 3:13-18; 1 Cor 3 18; Prov 11:2; Deut 12:32; Ecc 8:5-6; James 1:5; 1 Cor 2:6-16

Wisdom comes out of man's mind and his experience only; it is often merely expediency.

Interdependence—All subjects inc. PE
There is a theme of interdependence in the natural world and between people groups which, when valued, leads to enrichment and harmony.

1 Cor 12:12-27; Phil 2:1-4

We are autonomous, independent beings who may choose to co-operate with each other when it is in our own (self) interest.

Love and caring—Community and health care, PSHEE
We reflect God and his love by respecting people: this leads to concern and care for them.

Matt 22:37-39; James 2:8; Eph 5:1-2; 1 John 3:16-18

We may choose to care for others. Love is the expression of passion based on self-interest. Any covenants are optional, re-negotiable and often temporary.

Sharing resources—Geography
In a world where there is plenty but disparity, the willingness to share resources, which all come originally from God, will redress inequality of provision so all may benefit.

Gen 22:14; Ps 104; 1 Tim 6:17; 2 Cor 9:6-15; Rom 12:13; Acts 4:32-36

Earth's finite resources enhanced by man's creativity are all that are available: their use generates a conflict between conservation and self-interest.

Family—Sociology
The family is a foundational unit of society created by God who revealed himself as Father; it should be a positive environment for relationship and learning, including being honest and adhering to moral principles.

Gen 1:27-8; Eph 3:14-15

The world is comprised of autonomous ethnic groups and cultures; any family grouping is arbitrary.

Integrity—Moral values, PSHEE, citizenship
Integrity is the quality of being honest and living by strong moral principles;

the Bible provides God's principles for life as exemplified by Jesus Christ on earth.

Prov 11:3; Prov 3:1-8; 1 Tim 6:10

Humans live by their own individually chosen values as long as they do not contradict the democratic code of law at any given time.

Justice and Ethics — Law, moral issues, science, citizenship

Justice is the nature of God, rooted in his principles and is a foundational and integral desire for the fair treatment of all peoples.

Ps 9:8; Ps 72:2; Ps 89:14; Ps 96:13; Micah 6:8; Rom 3:21-26; Rev 16:7

Justice is the corporate decision of a people at any given time.

Communication — English lang., MFL, media studies

God is a communicating God. Communication in a digital age still needs to be accurate, clear and honest if good relationships are to be fully developed and maintained.

John 1:1-14; Eph 4:15; 2 Tim 3:16; Heb 1:1-2; 1 John 1:3-7

Communication is a means to an end for our self-satisfaction. A multiplicity of media (sources) enhances the quality of life.

Awe, wonder and worship — RE, art, music, astronomy, geography, science

Awe is an emotion of reverence, respect and wonder which is also an aspect of worship. Wonder is a response to something inspirational.

Job 37:14-24; Job chaps. 38-41; Exodus 15:11; Psalm 88:5; Ps 145: 3-5; Rom 11:33-36

We marvel at human and aspects of natural greatness and may worship humans and their achievement. Awe and wonder are frequently transitory unless based on evidence.

Culture, people and places — Anthropology, history, geography, art, music, drama

The study of culture (the customs, civilisation and achievements of peoples and societies) gives us deeper understanding of the purposes of God, who we are and how we belong.

Daniel chap. 7; Ps 8:3-5; Acts 17:24-31; Rev 7:9

The study of culture is purely based on personal interest or curiosity.

Growth and productivity — biology, economics, agriculture, business, RE

Everything which has life is created to grow to maturity and fruitfulness.

Ps 1:3; Ps 92:12-15; Matt 13:1-9, 23; Luke 16:8-13; Luke 14:28-32; John 15:5; Eph 4:15-16

Self-advancement is a dominant motivation for life but is not intrinsically related to maturity or fruitfulness.

Government and citizenship — politics, citizenship, history

Man is made in the image of God to govern; government should be exercised justly for the good of the people in that society.

Gen 1:28; Rom 13:1-7; Prov 12:24; Eph 6:1-2; Matt 28:18-20; Heb 13:7; Prov 18:5

Governments, whether autocratic or democratic, essentially serve selfish interests.

War, peace and reconciliation — history, world politics, current issues, PSHEE

Conflict between peoples requires diplomacy, mediation and mutual understanding to bring about the reconciliation and peace that God desires. The defence of justice and the oppressed may mean that war results where diplomacy breaks down.

2 Cor 5:18-21; Dan 9:26; Is 2:1-4; Heb 12:14; 1 Tim 2:1-2; Ps 34:14; Zech 9:10

Man's ability can resolve conflict: war is always undesirable and unnecessary.

The future — RE, ecology, science, geography, future trends

The future belongs to those who prepare for it; the study of God's word and his ways help us to be ready for what may come.

Prov 21:30; Matt 7:24-29; Jer 29:11

A positive future can be secured by economic provision but it cannot be predicted.

Beliefs — RE, theology, world religions, philosophy
Belief is a trust, faith or confidence which needs to be examined and considered. Faith in God is a gift from him.

Heb 11:1; Heb 11:6; John 3:1-21; Hab 2:4; Rom 10:17; James 2:14; Eph 2:8, Psalm 14:1

Beliefs are irrelevant unless substantiated by evidence.

KEYMFL — Modern Foreign Languages

PSHEE — Personal, Social, Health and Economic Education

21 Truths for Early Years

1. Uniqueness — Genesis 1:27-28, 1 Peter 1:18-19. Father God has made us each special.
2. Creation — Genesis 1:1, John 1. Father God has made a wonderful world.
3. Protection — Psalm 33:6-11, Job 42:2, Acts 17:26. Father God, Jesus and the Holy Spirit look after us.
4. Unity and diversity — 1 Corinthians 12, Romans 12:3-8. We can play and work as a team if we each play our part.
5. Order — Genesis 1, Isaiah 9:7a, 1 Corinthians 14:33. Each number and letter has a place to be and so do we.
6. Wisdom — Proverbs 2:1-4; 4:7-8, Colossians 2:2-3. God can help us make good choices.
7. Interdependence — Ecclesiastes 4:9-12, Galatians 6:2, 1 Corinthians 12. We need each other.
8. Unconditional love — Exodus 34:6-7, John 3:16, 1 John 3:1. God loves me whatever I do: I can love God.
9. Great Commission — Matthew 28:18-20, Acts 1:8. We can tell others

about God's love.

10. Fatherhood and family—Ephesians 3:14-15, Genesis 1:27-28. God is a good father: we are all his family.

11. Stewardship and servanthood—Genesis 1:26, Luke 19:11-27, John 13:2-17, Philippians 2. We can help each other and take care of our things.

12. Righteousness—Psalm 89:14, Psalm 119:137, Isaiah 9:7, Romans 14:17. We can learn what is right and what is wrong.

13. Justice—2 Chronicles 12:6, Psalm 89:14, Revelation 19:1-2. God always does what is right.

14. Provision and Resources—Gen 22:14; Ps 104; 1 Tim 6:17. Father God will give us what we need.

15. Communication—John 1:1-14, Ephesians 4:15, 2 Timothy 3:16, Hebrews 1:1-2, 1 John 1:3,7. We can speak and write, draw and paint.

16. Wonder-worship—Psalm 8, Job chap 37-42, Daniel 4:3, Romans 11:35-36. Father God loves us to sing to him.

17. Placement—Deuteronomy 32:8, Acts 17:26. God wants us all to have a place to live.

18. Growth, Maturity, Fruitfulness—Psalm 1:3, Psalm 92:12-15, Matthew 13:1-9, 23, John 15:5, Ephesians 4:15-16. Everything grows big and makes seeds.

19. Governing—Ruling Genesis 1:28, Matthew 28:18-20, Romans 13:1-5, Ephesians 6:1-2, Hebrews 13:17. Teacher is in charge when I am here.

20. Forgiveness, Reconciliation—Exodus 34:6, Matthew 18:21-35, Ephesians 2:13-16. We can say 'sorry' or 'I forgive you' when things go wrong.

21. Eternity, Infinity—Psalm 90:1-4, Ecclesiastes 3:11, John 17:3, 2 Timothy 1-10. We can live forever with Jesus and Father God.

Appendix 3 — Keys for Wisdom in Curriculum

21 Principles for Early Years (for More General Use)

1. Uniqueness—We are each special and different.
2. The World—We live in a wonderful world.
3. Protection—We need to protect each other.
4. Unity and Diversity—We are all different but we can work as a team if we each play our part.
5. Order—Each number and letter has a place to be and so do we.
6. Wisdom—Parents, carers and teachers can help us make good choices.
7. Interdependence—We need each other.
8. Love—Our parents, carers and teachers are meant to accept us and care for us.
9. Sharing—It is good to share and be friendly with others
10. Family—We are part of a larger family in our school.
11. Stewardship and Servanthood—We can help each other and take care of our things.
12. Right choices—We can learn to choose what is right and not what is wrong.
13. Justice—We learn to do what is right and treat others the way we would like to be treated.
14. Provision and Resources—We can ask for what we need.
15. Communication—We can speak and write, draw and paint.
16. Wonder—There are many things in the world which can cause us to wonder and ask questions.
17. Placement—We are all meant to have a place to live.
18. Growth, Maturity and Fruitfulness—Every plant grows bigger and makes seeds.
19. Governing—Ruling Teacher is in charge when I am here.

20. Forgiveness and Reconciliation—We can say 'sorry' or 'I forgive you' when things go wrong.
21. Beyond Us—The universe is very big and there are things to find out when we are older which are too big for us to understand now.

The Way to Wisdom Curriculum Model

Jesus said, *"I am the way, the truth and the life. No one comes to the Father except through me" (John 14:6).* The following model could be used as a guide for our thinking and planning:

- ◊ Truth to Teach
- ◊ Way to Work
- ◊ Learning for Life

Truth to Teach

Our aim in Christian Education is for children to know Jesus as their Lord, the One who is the embodiment of truth, the Lord who gives direction and purpose to life.

We pray about the truths we wish to impart to our pupils that may include:-

Heart concept

The opposing lie

Other concepts

Way to Work

Jesus is the most effective teacher who used many different ways of teaching the truth.

'In Him are all the treasures of wisdom and knowledge.' Colossians 2:3

The Way is the methodology, the way we are going to teach the lesson:

- ◊ Review of previous lesson, if appropriate
- ◊ Introduction
- ◊ Class, group, individual teaching
- ◊ Visual aids
- ◊ Progression of teaching concepts, activities
- ◊ Review of lesson

Learning for Life (Wisdom)
This involves two aspects: Understanding and Application.

Understanding: (Do they know it?)
1. The content of the lesson—the new facts or skills taught
2. The concept/seed of truth

Application: (extended questions to see if they can apply it)
Where else can we see this truth in God's creation?

1. How does this apply in my life? What does it mean for me?
2. Is there a wider application of the teaching beyond the subject?

Planning a Lesson on the Water Cycle

Truth to Teach
Heart Concept: The water cycle shows God's wise and economic provision. Ecclesiastes 1:7

The opposing lie: The water cycle is a random evolutionary procedure

Other Concepts: To learn about the processes of condensation and evaporation and how these enable water to be recycled

Way to Work
Progressive steps of the lesson. Visual aids.

Learning for Life (Wisdom)
Understanding:

1. Do the pupils understand how the water cycle works and the new vocabulary?
2. Do the pupils recognise God's wisdom in recycling water?

Application:

They can see where else in creation God uses a re-cycling process: plants and seeds; caterpillar to butterfly etc.

They can say how this affects their lives and people of other nations with a different water cycle e.g. deserts.

Appendix 3 — Keys for Wisdom in Curriculum

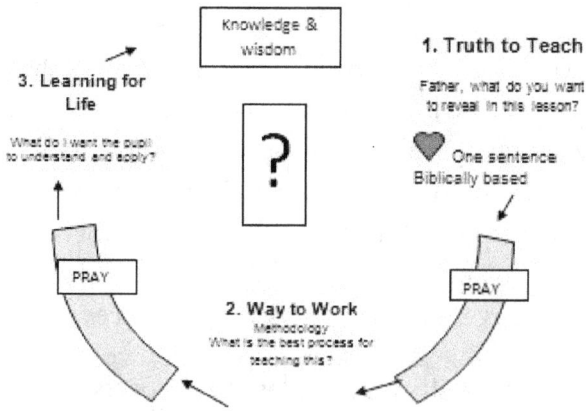

Planning a Lesson on Verb Tenses

Truth to Teach
Heart Concept: 'Jesus is the same yesterday and today and for ever.' Hebrews 13:8

Opposing lie: Verb tenses were developed by man

Other Concepts: The three tenses of a verb are past, present and future.

Way to Work
Progressive steps of the lesson

Visual aids

Learning for Life (Wisdom)
Understanding:

1. The pupils understand and can use the three tenses accurately.
2. The pupils have understood that Jesus remains the same in every age: past, present and future.

Application:

Can the pupils find ways in which God remains the same throughout the Bible?

How does this apply in their life of faith?

Applying the 21 Truths to Specific Curriculum

Note that the 21 concepts are major heart concepts and each has many different aspects which can be highlighted using different words and different ways in order to give you the particular heart concept(s) you need in the Way to Wisdom model approach. I would see these 21 as an umbrella under which all other lesson heart concepts can fit. We need to ask God for creative ways to use the concepts, avoiding slavish repetition of the sentences as written which can cause a boring familiarity for the students which will breed contempt.

Questions to be answered during the planning process:

- ◊ Which of the following 21 concepts apply to this particular aspect of curriculum? Note: there are 7 of the 21 which apply in different ways to every aspect of the curriculum.
- ◊ Do I want to use all of the relevant concepts? Note: the answer to 1b depends on the other lesson/themes being taught in the class in other areas of curriculum. The teacher needs to make value judgements about how much to emphasise well-used concepts (like the major 7) or whether merely to draw attention to them in passing.
- ◊ Pray: what aspects does God want to emphasise—TRUTH TO TEACH. In this way clarify and prioritise the heart concept(s) you will major on.
- ◊ Which are the lies to oppose? See list of false beliefs in our culture.
- ◊ How (in what ways) do the relevant heart concepts apply to this curriculum? WAY TO WORK.
- ◊ How shall I lead the students to discover and then examine the relevant lies and truths? WAY TO WORK.
- ◊ How and what do I want the students to understand and apply? LEARNING FOR LIFE.

Appendix 3 — Keys for Wisdom in Curriculum

LESSON PLAN

Year/Class Group(s): _____

Subject/Topic: _____

TRUTH TO TEACH (Which of the 21 Truths may apply?)
_____

Heart Concept:
(1 sentence biblically based)

Opposing Lie

Other Concepts

WAY TO WORK

Learning for Life (WISDOM)

Post-lesson assessment

Appendix 4

Outline Truths for Use in Lessons Based on the Way to Wisdom Model

In this sample of lesson outlines we are looking at the TRUTH to teach section of the model structure which involves the heart truth ie the truth at the heart of the lesson. This might be called our main objective. It will come first in your lesson objectives.

In addition this sample illustrates how understanding and application, which are the third part of the model, the LIFE/WISDOM part can be written.

REMEMBER: We need to PRAY before planning; we are teachers who depend on the Holy Spirit to guide us.

- ◊ Pray: Which of the 21 Truths apply best? Choose the best for your lesson.
- ◊ Pray: From that one which has been chosen, which words should I choose for my heart truth sentence so that it focuses on the lesson topic and so that the children of my class will read and understand at their own level?
- ◊ Pray: Use the Word of God; select a scripture to go with your heart truth sentence. It may be one on the list of 21 Truths or one to which the Holy Spirit will quicken you.

Remember numbers 1-7 of the 21 apply to every subject of the curriculum in different ways. God can also direct us to any of the others.

The following are some sample ideas for lessons. These are to encourage you but do not just copy them — remember to pray. God may change it for your class!

MATHS

Lesson 1: Counting 1 to 10
This is about sequence which is a part of Order: Number 5 of the 21 Truths

TRUTH

Heart truth: God made numbers and gave each one a right place.

Other concepts: E.g. number recognition, sequence and position.

Lie: Numbers are man-made.

LIFE/WISDOM

Understanding: Who made numbers and what is the order for 1–10? Tell your partner the number order for 5–10.

Application: In what sports are number positions important? Why?

Lesson 2: Sets—an introduction to multiplication for young children
Growth and Fruitfulness: Number 18 of the 21 Truths

TRUTH

Heart truth: God gives us quick ways to add (Proverbs 8:33) and likes multiplying (Gen 1: 28 RSV).

Other concepts: E.g. sets—how multiplication is continued addition.

Lie: Multiplication is man's cleverness.

LIFE/WISDOM

Understanding: That X is quicker than adding if we learn tables. Explain to your partner the X sign in maths. Why is it quicker than adding?

Application: Practise your 1 and 2 times tables. What else can X mean?

Lesson 3: Fractions

Interdependence: Number 7 of the 21 Truths

TRUTH

Heart truth: Everything in God's world is created to be part of something larger (1 Corinthians 12: 27).

Other concepts: E.g. a fraction is a part of a whole; only equal-sized fractions have names. ½ means 1 of 2 equal parts.

Lie: Fractions are man's invention; we are all independent individuals.

LIFE/WISDOM

Understanding: Tell your partner what a fraction means and explain how you are each a fraction as well as a whole person (1 Cor 12: 27).

Application: Find as many things as you can in your home from which fractions can be made.

Note: An alternative could be to teach fractions teaching Fatherhood and Family which is number 10 in which case the heart truth could be 'Everyone in God's world is a whole person and a fraction.' Psalm 68:6

Lesson 4: Subtraction

Sovereignty of God: Number 3 of the 21 Truths

TRUTH

Heart truth: God may prune or 'take away' when we don't use what he has given or it is no longer needed (John 15: 2, John 1: 29).

Other concepts: E.g. the meaning of the subtraction sign. How to subtract tens and units.

Lie: Subtraction is man's idea and has no meaning other than a mathematical one.

LIFE/WISDOM

Understanding: How to subtract numbers. Is subtraction a good or a bad thing? (Note: it can be either!)

Application: Tell your partner the right way to subtract the sum 21-9. God can take away sin. You may want to talk to the teacher if you need God to take sin away from your life.

NB An alternative heart truth could be: "God takes away what is not needed, e.g. sin".

Lesson 5: Division
Justice: Number 13 of the 21 Truths

TRUTH

Heart truth: When we are sharing something with others, God cares about each one having the same (Ps 89:14).

Other concepts: The process of division with single numbers, then larger.

Lie: We decide what is just, without God.

LIFE/WISDOM

Understanding: The process of division. God shares his blessings with us. Why is unequal sharing not fair?

Application: List the things you can share equally at home or school. Can you remember a time when someone received something but you did not? How did it make you feel?

Note: An alternative heart truth could be forgiveness and reconciliation, Number 20 of the 21 Truths.

Lesson 6: Secondary Lesson on Equations
Reconciliation: Number 20 of the 21 Truths

TRUTH

Heart truth: In equations, God enables us to balance or reconcile both sides (Matthew 18:21-35).

Other concepts: How to set out and process equations.

Lie: We can do this without God; it has nothing to do with Him.

LIFE/WISDOM

Understanding: Explain to your partner the process for solving and reconciling and equation. How did God reconcile us to Himself?

Application: How many jobs or activities in life involve reconciling or balancing things? Make a list. Are there things you need to deal with God over to bring reconciliation with someone or something?

English or any Language Teaching
Primary 6 or Secondary

Lesson 1: Introduction to Language
(Primary 4-6 level)
Communication: Number 15 of the 21 Truths, and Sovereignty: Number 3 of 21

TRUTH

Heart truth: People in different countries speak different languages because God created different languages (Genesis 11).

Other concepts: (From set national curriculum for this lesson)

Lie: Different languages just developed through man's cleverness.

LIFE/WISDOM

Understanding: Language concepts taught. In the sovereignty of God I was born in _____ so I speak _____. Explain to your partner why there are different languages in different countries and decide how many.

Application: What languages can you speak? Use them to write a sentence in 2 or 3 languages. Are there going to be different languages in heaven?

Lesson 2: Language
The Sovereignty of God: Number 3 of the 21 Truths

TRUTH

Heart truth: God created different languages to limit sinful man from uniting in order to do greater evil (Genesis 11:1-9, the story of Babel).

Other concepts: The structure of a sentence in the language chosen.

Lie: Different languages just developed through man's cleverness.

LIFE/WISDOM

Understanding: Sentence structure in the chosen language. How do different languages limit sin? Look up Genesis 11:6.

Application: Can you think of a story in an early chapter of the book of Acts which reverses this pattern? Why did God do this?

Lesson 3: Introduction to Nouns
(Primary level)
Order: Number 5 of the 21 Truths

TRUTH

Heart truth: Nouns are naming words; God used the first nouns to name things and give order (Genesis 1:5, 8, 10). Story idea: Adam naming the animals (Genesis 2:20).

Other concepts: E.g. common and proper nouns and which is which.

Lie: Nouns are names made up by man.

LIFE/WISDOM

Understanding: Tell your partner why a noun is different to other words.

Application: With your partner, find five common and five proper nouns in the classroom. Remember: your name is also a special noun called a 'proper noun'.

Lesson 4: Punctuation
Communication: Number 15 of the 21 Truths, and Order: Number 5 of the 21

TRUTH

Heart truth: By using correct punctuation we communicate more clearly what we mean; in this way we are like God.

Other concepts: E.g. the full stop, comma etc and when to use them.

Lie: Punctuation is man's invention.

LIFE/WISDOM

Understanding: . . . Tell your partner what punctuation is and why it is important. Explain the use of a full stop and comma.

Application: Punctuate these sentences in different ways (give a set to work with).

Lesson 5: Adjectives
(Primary 4-6 level)
Made in God's image: Number 1 of the 21 Truths

TRUTH

Heart truth: Adjectives are describing words which help us to 'see' more with our imagination, like God does (Genesis 1:27-28).

Other concepts: e.g. How to use them.

Lie: Adjectives are to do with man's creativity.

LIFE/WISDOM

Understanding: Underline the adjectives in a sentence your teacher gives you or look in a book and count the adjectives on a page. Tell your partner how clear communication makes us more like God.

Application: Describe your friend's appearance using good adjectives without using your friend's name. Then test your writing by letting others read it and guess who you are describing.

Lesson 6: Tenses
The Sovereignty of God: Number 3 of the 21 Truths

TRUTH

Heart truth: We live in time which has a past, present and future but God is always present tense (Exodus 3:14, story of the burning bush).

Other concepts: E.g. How to recognise the three tenses and when to use them. How they affect verbs in a sentence.

Lie: God does not exist in any tense or time.

LIFE/WISDOM

Understanding: Practise putting sentences into a different tense. Say which tense God lives in.

Application: Tell your partner the story of the burning bush in the present tense as if you were Moses (Exodus 3).

Appendix 4 — Outline Truths for Use in Lessons

Science

Lesson 1: Classification
Order: Number 5 of the 21 Truths

TRUTH

Heart truth: God created classification when he made the universe; it is the way to bring order to the many things in God's world (I Kings 4:29-34, the story of Solomon, especially verse 33).

Other concepts: E.g. the way to label and classify types or 'kinds'.

Lie: Classification is man's idea.

LIFE/WISDOM

Understanding: Explain classification in Genesis 1 to your partner; look especially at verses 11 and 12.

Application: Classify some types of creatures you might find in your country.

Lesson 2: Disease
Creator and Creation: Number 2 of the 21 Truths

TRUTH

Heart truth: There is disease in God's world because of the fall of Adam and Eve, but God is our healer and also provides cures through plants and medicines (Exodus 15:26).

Other concepts: E.g. what causes disease.

Lie: Disease is nothing to do with sin or God; it is only a result of certain processes.

LIFE/WISDOM

Understanding: Discuss with your partner why Adam and Eve caused disease to come to the earth.

Application: Give a testimony of when God healed you or list healing plants or medicines that you know of. Is anyone sick or absent today from your class? Pray for them.

Lesson 3: The Prevention of Disease
Wisdom: Number 6 of the 21 Truths

TRUTH

Heart truth: We are responsible for our bodies. We can help prevent disease by keeping our bodies clean and eating and drinking clean things (2 Corinthians 7:1).

LIFE/WISDOM

Understanding: List the ways you can protect yourselves from disease.

Application: Give a testimony of when God healed you or list healing plants or medicines that you know of. How can we prevent malaria? Or write a prayer for healing your sick brother/sister or friend.

Lesson 4: The Lifecycle of any Insect or Creature
(Primary 5 to secondary)
Growth and Fruitfulness: Number 18 of the 21 Truths

TRUTH

Heart truth: God has designed (name of creature) for growth, and he has designed you to grow too.

Other concepts: E.g. How the creature grows and matures its lifecycle.

Lie: Everything grows because of biology not because of God.

LIFE/WISDOM

Understanding: Tell your partner how the lifecycle works.

Application: God wants you to grow physically, mentally, emotionally and spiritually. Pray about some ways in which you want to grow.

Note: An alternative approach to this lesson could be to use Wisdom Number 6 of the 21 Truths and to use the scripture ref. Romans 11:33 and write a heart truth to do with God's wisdom in the life cycle.

Lesson 5: Pollution of Environment
(Primary or Secondary)
Stewardship and servant-hood: Number 11 of the 21 Truths

TRUTH

Heart truth: Man has polluted/spoiled God's creation by his selfishness and carelessness; we should not be selfish and careless (Philippians 2:3-4).

Other concepts: E.g. causes of pollution and ways to prevent or clean up pollution.

Lie: Pollution is sometimes the result of man's progress—we should control it where if affects our future.

LIFE/WISDOM

Understanding: Talk with your partner about how God wanted us to be a good steward (Genesis 1 and 2).

Application: What types of pollution happen in your town, village or home? What could you do to improve your environment?

Lesson 6: Photosynthesis
(Secondary)
Worship: Number 16 of the 21 Truths

TRUTH

Heart truth: Photosynthesis is God's wonderful plan to enable a plant to go on growing (Romans 11:33, how wonderful are your ways, O God!).

Other concepts: E.g. how photosynthesis takes place.

Lie: Photosynthesis is a part of the process of evolution.

LIFE/WISDOM

Understanding: Explain how photosynthesis works and try to spell the word correctly.

Application: Do our bodies need the same ingredients as plants? Give thanks for God's wonderful ways in nature.

Note: Alternative: Provision & Resources, Number 14 of the 21 Truths

God has provided food for us through plants making food from the sun's energy.

Application: Thank God for this provision. What other provision has he made? (land to live on, water to drink etc).

Social Studies

Lesson 1: A Country's geographical position (Secondary)
Placement: Number 17 of the 21 Truths

TRUTH

Heart truth: Acts 17:26 God created (your country) to be a land which has the following physical features: (list).

Other concepts: E.g. position of your country in its continent and the boundaries and physical features.

Lie: Your country just evolved; no one created it.

LIFE/WISDOM

Understanding: (Our country) is positioned where God planned—we should be thankful.

Application: . . . . In what ways can (your country) help her neighbours and in what ways can they help your country? Which physical features in your country are a special blessing?

Lesson 2: Safety in the Home (Secondary)
Wisdom: Number 6 of the 21 Truths

TRUTH

Heart truth: God wants us to be wise: we must think ahead and plan our steps, especially if we want to prevent unnecessary accidents (Proverbs 14: 15 prudent = wise, Isaiah 46:10).

Other concepts: e.g. Dangers in the home and ways to prevent accidents.

Lie: Safety is just common sense.

LIFE/WISDOM

Understanding: Parents and older brothers and sisters must think ahead and prevent danger. Who can help us to think ahead?

Application: Look in your home and/or compound and try to see what may be dangerous. What can you do to make it safer? Think and pray about your future. Ask God to help you plan your steps.

Lesson 3: Government
(Secondary)
Governing and Ruling: Number 19 of the 21 Truths

TRUTH

Heart truth: Governments represent God's authority on earth: they exist because He permits them; they are meant to govern justly (Romans 13:1).

Other concepts: E.g. explore issues of justice and how God may be involved in the democratic process.

Lie: Governments represent man's authority and are elected by man.

LIFE/WISDOM

Understanding: We are to respect government because God permits it for a season but we must obey God when governments do not obey God's laws (Acts 4:19).

Application: Because governments are permitted by God we should pray for them (1 Timothy 2:1). With a partner, pray now for your government to act justly and for Christians to be elected.

Lesson 4: Agricultural tools
(Primary)
Created in God's Image: Number 21 of the 21 Truths

TRUTH

Heart truth: God has made us like him so that we can think of ways to create new tools to help us in agriculture (Genesis 1:28-29, Exodus 35: 30-35).

Other concepts: E.g. useful tools

Lie: Man creates new tools from his own cleverness.

LIFE/WISDOM

Understanding: We can picture and plan new inventions to improve our work because we are made like God.

Application: . . . . Try to think of better ways to do some of your tasks in the garden or home, or design a new tool to make agricultural or other tasks easier.

Appendix 5
Unconditional Acceptance

Effective teaching, we believe, is based on a relationship of unconditional acceptance of pupils by the teacher. This relationship involves encouragement and affirmation. The Christian values of forgiveness and grace are vital in any inclusion agenda.

What is unconditional acceptance?

It receives another person just as he or she is, without criticism or judgement. It raises no legal barriers; it says, "I accept you; you count."[1] This acceptance on a relational level—according dignity and value to a person—is not based on what they can do; their social status or how they look, but on the basis of them being a human being intrinsically worthy of respect.

Acceptance is recognised as a basic human need for everyone. For those pupils who are insecure, or lacking in confidence or ability, acceptance is the first foundation for their learning. Without it they may never make progress no matter how much finance or technology is provided for them. Psychologists agree that tension or fear blocks learning by affecting the emotional pathways. Acceptance provides confidence. Ross Campbell, a counsellor of thousands of troubled teenagers,[2] has discovered that the common question, whether spoken or unspoken, is: 'Do I matter?' They are asking if they count, not on the basis of ability, or grades or behaviour—but as a person.

Increasing the learning potential

Acceptance is the first building block of forming a relationship. Every good teacher or youth worker knows that you can get further with a young person if they know you care about them and a relational connection is established. Often children or young people know instinctively whether a person is for them or has another agenda; this includes their parents. Vygotsky, a Russian psychologist,[3]

---
1 E.J. Carnell: The Kingdom of Love and the Pride of Life p.7
2 Ross Campbell: Loving Your Teen.
3 Lev Vygotsky

believes in what he called 'cooperative or collaborative dialogue'.[4] He proved through testing, that with relational encouragement, whether by a peer or a teacher, the amount of learning that can take place will be enhanced. He named the zone of extra learning the zone of proximal development—or 'the zpd factor.'

Some Victorian teaching majored on the imposition of fear, criticism and public shaming, as is still the case in some cultures today. This causes lasting damage. Not only this, but such an approach disaffects the pupil from learning that subject. I have asked countless teachers about their favourite subjects and the subjects they dislike. In many, many cases the factor causing affection or disaffection for a subject, was the teacher and the type of relationship or non-relationship formed.

Case Study

Doug started at Grammar school at the age of 11, having been 2nd in the class for maths and quite enjoying it. He encountered a different syllabus which took no account of the primary schools curriculum and a cynical and sarcastic teacher who systematically humiliated and shamed all who could not achieve quickly. Doug's confidence was destroyed and by the end of the 1st year he came 32nd in a class of 34!! ... And he hated Maths from then on and never achieved an exam pass in the subject.

Unconditional acceptance is mainly expressed through kindness. Doug's teacher lacked this basic component! The first act of kindness is to show each child that you accept them as a person, regardless of their ability. This meets a foundational human need. Kindness is further expressed when we show grace for pupils' imperfections and their failures to fulfil requirements or expectations—even in mundane but important matters such as looking after their own property or that of the school.

Too many teachers have forgotten what it was like to be a child or teenager. They need to do as Atticus Finch, the lawyer father, encouraged his children to do in 'To Kill a Mocking Bird'—'to put themselves in another's shoes'.[5] In this way, understanding and a measure of compassion is aroused in the teacher/leader, and

---

4   Mcleod S. A. (2007) Simply Psychology. www.simplypsychology.org/vygotsky.html
5   Harper Lee: To Kill a Mockingbird p.30

with it, more grace and patience.

Positive components needed in the teacher or youth-worker relationship:

The relationship forged between the personal coach and the young athlete is a good example of the powerful effect of a positive teacher-student relationship. The film, 'Chariots of Fire' depicts this in the true story of aspiring Jewish athlete, Harold Abrahams who submits himself to the training of coach, Sam Mussabini. This leads to the unlocking of greater potential than the young man had shown before. The coach provided a bedrock of acceptance for Abrahams and spoke out his confidence that his young pupil could achieve his dream, which he did.

Patience, kindness, humour, encouragement, praise, perseverance. reward, consideration, forgiveness; the ability to inspire hope and expressions of faith in the young person by the teacher/leader builds them up. Cutting comments, sarcasm or anger are destructive and disable the young person, rather than encouraging them. Partiality is another factor which creates a negative 'spin' in a class or group. As soon as young people discern favouritism they react against the injustice and are de-motivated.

Examples of inspiring teachers

The teacher who has vision for a student can impart it to them and lead them in to it—without a vision, leader and follower will not achieve and may drift aimlessly. The following pay tribute to their inspiring teachers:

Paddy Ashdown, (Politician)

John Eyre really changed my life. He persuaded me to join the poetry society (which all rugby playing "hearties" resolutely despised) and gave me a lifetime love of poetry, even getting me to write some for the school magazine. Eyre lit in me a fire for literature, especially Shakespeare, which has never gone out. (www.guardian.co.uk/education/2010/jan)

Mr. Glaze (Maths Teacher) West Potomac High School in Alexandria, VA

He has inspired me both in the classroom and outside in the world. Math is normally a class many students dread. This teacher, on the other hand, taught me to enjoy math and see the real world connections in each problem. He taught problem solving skills that can be used in any situation. He also pushed me to succeed. While some teachers will give up on a struggling student, he works with each and every student in order to help them thrive and fully understand the subject… His strength inspires me in everything I do. He is truly a great teacher with the ability to inspire anyone. (Alexandra Butler age 16, grade 11)

Andrew Motion (Former Poet Laureate)

My background was very unbookish, and there was absolutely no expectation from my family of my ever reading very much or even writing anything. …Then I was taught English by Peter Way (Mr. Way to me), and it was as though he walked into my head and turned all the lights on. (www.guardian.co.uk/education/2010/jan)

Michael Morpurgo, (Author)

The teacher who most inspired me was Edred Wright, director of music at the King's School, Canterbury. His great gift was being able to inspire children (like me) who weren't necessarily musically gifted—that's what we should require of teachers in all subjects. With Mr. Wright it was never about improving the reputation of the school, just his intense love of music. What that man taught me aged 14 has enriched my entire life. (www.guardian.co.uk/education/2010/jan)

Jesus Christ is acknowledged world-wide as the most effective teacher. The fruit of his teaching means that there are estimated to be over 2 billion followers in the world today.[6] His approaches always involved relational acceptance and respect for the individual. He treated people as they would like to be treated. He taught the 'golden rule' of love: 'So in everything do to others what you would have them do to you.' [7]

His closest pupils were taught through a variety of methods, nearly all involving a

---

6   Global Christianity: A Report on the size and distribution of the world's Christian population in: www.pew forumonreligion.co.uk
7   The Bible; Matthew's Gospel Chapter 7:12

mentoring relationship. At HighLight we have explored and used many of these methods successfully.

Unconditional acceptance as the channel for teaching

This acceptance is a medium (channel) of knowledge because it opens the heart of the learner to receive. Intellectualism often refuses to accept this as a medium of knowledge. 'Philosophers may disagree about many things, but they agree that there is only one medium of knowledge, and that is a critically disciplined intellect…This assumes that intellectual detachment has access to all available information. But, in truth, the most important information, that which involves the secrets of the heart, remains inaccessible until detachment gives way to fellowship. This is a rule to which there is no exception.'[8] The more we express loving acceptance to a person, the more they will trust us and be able to receive from us.

The harassed teacher may be saying 'This is all very well—but you don't teach my class!' The truth is that it is hard to accept and care for all pupils and, as none of us are perfect, we will not find it easy to maintain a loving approach throughout the varied experiences of the day, which sometimes includes irate parents! When he was on earth, Jesus ran out of strength just as we do and needed to renew it by time with his Father. From a Christian perspective it is possible to find grace for all our students by the enabling power of the Holy Spirit. If we will ask, we will receive.[9]

Unconditional acceptance as corrective discipline

However this sort of 'love', which Jesus demonstrated, is not a soft option: it is 'loving' to correct and to discipline. The Bible makes it clear that correction is part of loving in the process of bringing our children to maturity. It may involve loss of privilege or punishment of some kind as a consequence of wrong choices.

'No discipline is pleasant at the time, but painful. Later on, however, it produces a harvest of righteousness and peace for those who have been trained by it.'[10]

---

8 E.J. Carnell: The Kingdom of Love and The Pride of Life p.49
9 The Bible: Luke's Gospel Chapter 11:13
10 The Bible; Hebrews Chapter 12: 11

Whilst correction is needed it must be redemptive and motivated by a love which has vision for the pupil's potential character formation.

Of course, there will need to be rebuke, correction and a crossing of the will at times. But if the right to do this has been earned, it will be more easily accepted (although never popular at the time!). It also functions with greater success where there has grown a bond of mutual respect.

Appendix 6
Keys for Wisdom in Character

"I have a dream that my four little children will one day live in a nation where they will not be judged by the color of their skin but by the content of their character."
— *Martin Luther King*

Desirable character qualities need to be taught and encouraged. Someone once said, 'Gifting without character is like a gem in a loose setting: it is easily lost.'

The following is HighLight's suggested qualities for attaining wisdom in character.

Desirable Qualities for Attaining Wisdom in Character

- ◊ Diligent—Luke 16:10-12; 1 Cor 4:2; Heb 6:10-12. *I give my best effort to all that I do.*
- ◊ Responsible—John 14:1; Prov 3:5. *I am willing to take responsibility.*
- ◊ Humble—Psalm 119:11; Prov 8:13; Rom 12:9, 21, 1 John 3:3-9. *I am honest about my strengths and weaknesses.*
- ◊ Attentive—Isa 50:4-5, Matt 7:24-29. *I actively listen.*
- ◊ Responsive—John 14:23, 1 John 5:3. *I follow learning instructions.*
- ◊ Team player—Rom 12:4-5, 1 Cor 12:25-27. *I opt in to working with others.*
- ◊ Caring—John 13:34, Rom 12:10. *I take opportunities to care for others.*
- ◊ Teachable—Micah 6:8, Rom 12:3. *I am willing to go on learning.*
- ◊ Globally aware—Matt 6:33, Eph 2:10. *I am part of something bigger than myself.*
- ◊ Forgiving—Rom 12:17-20. *I don't hold grudges.*
- ◊ Integrity—Ps 51:6, Prov 12:22. *I hold positive values and live by them.*
- ◊ Inclusive—Phil 2:3-4. *I accept and welcome people who are different to me.*

- ◊ Generous—Luke 6:38, Heb 13:16. *I share what I can.*
- ◊ Respectful—Rom 13:1, Titus 3:1. *I respect authority.*
- ◊ Courageous—Ps 82:3, Josh 1:7. *I will defend what is right.*
- ◊ Problem-solving—Ecc 8:5. *I try to bring solutions.*
- ◊ Reliable—Eph. 6:15. I am dependable.
- ◊ Fair—Micah 6:8, 1 John 3:7. *I will protect the rights of the marginalised and disadvantaged.*
- ◊ Self-controlled—1 Thess 2:10, 2 Tim 1:7. *I know my boundaries and keep them.*
- ◊ Patient—Rom 12:12, 1 Thess 5:14. *I can wait.*
- ◊ Positive—Rom 12:12, 1Tim 6:17. *I maintain a hope for the future.*
- ◊ Resilient—Matt 7:7-8, Heb 10:35-39, Phil 3:14. *I cope with challenges and don't give up.*
- ◊ Honest—Ps 51:6, Prov 12:22. *I am truthful.*
- ◊ Loyal—Prov 17:17. *I aim to maintain positive relationships even in hard times.*
- ◊ Adaptable—Matt 18:3. *I can embrace change.*
- ◊ Serving—Matt 4:10, Eph 6:7, John 13:14-17. *I do what I can to meet the needs of others.*
- ◊ Sense of humour—Ps 45:7, Heb 1:9. *I can laugh at myself and with others.*
- ◊ Perceptive—1 Kings 3:12. *I can assess different situations appropriately.*
- ◊ Wise—Prov 9:10, James 1:5; 3:13. *I can respond to different situations appropriately.*
- ◊ Self-acceptance—Ps 139:14. *I accept myself.*
- ◊ Consequential Thinking—Prov 16:9. *I consider the consequences of my choices and actions.*
- ◊ Consistent—Luke 16:10-12. *I am consistent in my work and behaviour.*

About the Author

David's career has largely focused on the education and discipling of children and the training of teachers. He was founding head of The King's School, Witney, Oxford, in 1984 where he was headteacher for 17 years. He has subsequently helped plant Christian schools in the UK, Kazakhstan, Poland, Uganda and Rwanda. He also now regularly trains teachers in these countries and has had input to Canada, Norway, India, Nigeria and some other African countries.

He mentors several teachers and also headteachers and other leaders in Rwanda, Uganda and S. Korea, where he recently spent 3 months and is Honorary Principal of a school in Seoul. In Rwanda he is regularly involved with pastors from Salt and Light International related churches in Rwanda. He is also one of 4 directors of Bridge Schools Inspectorate, which is officially recognised by the British government. He has set up HighLight (www.highlightonline.org) which aims to inspire and equip educators, offering key principles to help them be effective in their teaching and mentoring.

David is married to Rosie and they live in Henley-on-Thames. They have 3 children of their own, now married, and 11 grandchildren. They have also adopted an adult son in Rwanda who was an orphan.